National Power and the Structure of Foreign Trade

This is the first volume in a series The Politics of the International Economy, edited by Stephen D. Krasner, University of California, Los Angeles.

National Power and the Structure of Foreign Trade

By

ALBERT O. HIRSCHMAN

UNIVERSITY OF CALIFORNIA PRESS

BERKELEY, LOS ANGELES, LONDON

University of California Press
Berkeley and Los Angeles, California

University of California Press, Ltd.
London, England

Copyright © 1945 by
The Regents of the University of California
Expanded Edition copyright © 1980 by
The Regents of the University of California

ISBN 0–520–04082–1 paper
0–520–04084–8 cloth

Printed in the United States of America

1 2 3 4 5 6 7 8 9

Preface to the Expanded Edition

The suggestion to republish a little book that appeared more than thirty-five years ago and has been long out of print is uncommonly flattering to the book's author. But at the same time it presents him with a problem of conscience. It is only too clear that in such a long time not only has scholarship as such gone forward, but also the opinions of the author himself, even if fundamentally unchanged, have been altered in many details.

To take this development into account would be possible only if the author could bring himself to write a completely new book probably three or four times as big; but for this he lacks the time, the strength, and—to speak frankly—the inclination.

These sentences are from the foreword to the second edition of Erwin Panofsky's classic *Idea: A Concept in Art Theory* (New York: Harper & Row, 1924, 1960, 1968) and they are nicely and exactly—to the number of years—applicable to the present republishing venture. Any "updating" of this old essay of mine would indeed be a formidable undertaking. My main object of study was the politics of *foreign trade*, the possibility of using trade as a means of political pressure and leverage. During the first two decades of the postwar period, foreign aid and capital flows largely replaced trade as the principal arena for the political element in international economic relations.[1] More recently, with the negotiations at the United Nations Conferences on Trade and Development and the discussions about the New International Economic Order, trade and the institutional framework within which it is carried

---

[1] I have dealt with the politics of foreign aid in two articles which maintain, I believe, a certain continuity with the analysis of the present book: "The Stability of Neutralism" (1964) and "Foreign Aid: A Critique and a Proposal" (with Richard M. Bird, 1968), both reprinted in my *A Bias for Hope: Essays on Development and Latin America* (New Haven: Yale University Press, 1971).

on have come back into the picture. Time and inclination apart, an attempt to refurbish or modify the book's analytical tools so as to have them come to grips with these experiences could easily become an exercise in self-importance. But I recently had the occasion to return to the book with the simpler purpose of criticizing one of its features that has become unsatisfactory to me. The brief note that resulted is reproduced below.

ALBERT O. HIRSCHMAN
Princeton, May 1979

BEYOND ASYMMETRY:
CRITICAL NOTES ON MYSELF AS A YOUNG MAN AND
ON SOME OTHER OLD FRIENDS.[2]

"Dependency Theory Reassessed" was the title of the plenary session at the 1976 meetings of the Latin American Studies Association. In my remarks as session chairman I presented some of the speakers, such as Fernando Henrique Cardoso and Osvaldo Sunkel who were among the first to discuss "dependencia" in the early or mid-sixties, as the founding fathers of the theory. Then I proceeded to introduce myself as the frequently unacknowledged founding grandfather, on the strength of my book *National Power and the Structure of Foreign Trade* (1945). The point of this note, however, is not to substantiate this claim; it seems more useful to spell out my present critical perspective on that *Jugendschrift* of some 35 years ago (the manuscript was actually written in 1941–1942) and, in the process, to criticize as well some aspects of the dependencia literature.

The historical backdrop of my book was the successful drive of Hitler's Germany to expand its trade with, and its political influence in, Eastern and South-Eastern Europe during the thirties. In attempting to explain what had happened, I dwelt not so much on the diabolical cunning of the Nazis, or on Dr. Schacht's technical innovations such as bilateralism, exchange controls and so on, as on the structural characteristics of international economic relations that, as I wrote, "make the pursuit of power a relatively easy task."

───────────────

[2] Reproduced from *International Organization* 32 (Winter 1978), pp. 45–50, with minimal changes.

The Nazis, according to this point of view, had not perverted the international economic system, they had merely capitalized on one of its potentialities or side effects; for "power elements and dis- ⌉
equilibria are potentially inherent in such 'harmless' trade rela- ⌋
tions as have always taken place, e.g., between big and small, rich and poor, industrial and agricultural countries—relations that could be fully in accord with the principles taught by the theory of international trade" (p. 40).

It is of course this position which accounts for the durability of my book: the political dimensions and side effects of foreign trade and investment are still very much with us—two obvious examples are the relations of the United States with Latin America and of the Soviet Union with Eastern Europe.[3]

In forging a link between international economics and politics I focused primarily on the economic concept "gain from trade" and showed how, in line with the maxim *fortuna est servitus*, this gain can spell dependence of the country that receives the gain on the country that bestows it. Going along with the assumptions of classical theory, I assumed that both countries gain, but emphasized that in a large number of constellations, these gains are asymmetrical: a given volume of trade between countries A and B may be much more important for B than for A. A simple quantitative reflection of this asymmetry is present in the frequent case where a small, poor country (B) carries on a large portion of its trade with a large, rich country (A). In that case imports of A from B could well represent 80 percent of B's total exports while accounting for no more than 3 percent of A's total imports. I made a great deal of this and similar asymmetrics and disparities and devised various statistical instruments in an attempt to measure them.

So much for my grandfatherhood. Having explained how relations of influence, dependence, and domination arise right out of "mutually beneficial" trade I let matters rest there except for some, in retrospect infinitely naive, proposals to "arrive at an internationalization of the power arising out of foreign trade" (p. 80). In other words, I invoked a *deus ex machina*; I wished away the un-

---

[3] In the latter respect, an explicit use of my conceptual framework is in Paul Marer, "The Political Economy of Soviet Relations with Eastern Europe," in S. J. Rosen and J. R. Kurth, eds., *Testing Theories of Economic Imperialism* (Lexington, Mass.: Lexington Books, 1974), pp. 231–260.

pleasant reality I had uncovered instead of scrutinizing it further for some possibly built-in modifier or remedy. In this respect, my treatment had once again a great deal in common with that of many dependencia theorists: they, too, tend to rest content with the demonstration that dependency relations are deeply entrenched in the structure of the international system; they hardly ever explore whether that system might contain the "seeds of its own destruction" or might otherwise be subject to some changes. If they invoke revolution, it is also as a *deus ex machina*, rather than because they have identified any emerging forces capable of staging that desired event.

It may be instructive to indicate how this common defect of my original treatment and of most dependencia writings could be remedied by taking as point of departure the very situation of asymmetry previously noted: an identical trade flow that represents the bulk of the small, poor country's total trade while occupying only a small percentage of the large, rich country's trade. The straightforward inference from this observation is that the large country, having a much smaller stake in this common trade than the small country, is able to bend the latter to its will by subtle or not-so-subtle hints that the benefits of this trade might otherwise be withdrawn. But the next question is now: how solid or stable is the resulting relation of domination and dependency?

In his recent book, *Beyond Economic Man*, Harvey Leibenstein has reminded us of Tolstoy's critique, in *War and Peace*, of those military experts who predict the outcome of battles by looking only at the quantifiable elements of the strength of the opposing armies, such as the number of men and weapons—Tolstoy stresses fighting spirit and morale as an often more decisive factor. This thought has an obvious relevance here. The ability to inflict deprivation is more easily quantified than the willingness to accept it for the sake of, say, freedom from domination, and in the recent past there have been several important episodes where this willingness has been underestimated, with disastrous results for those who thought that "objectively" they were bound to prevail.

While this factor—the willingness to accept economic (or physical) punishment—must be taken into account in assessing the stability of the dependence relationship, one cannot count on it. To do so would again be tantamount to invoking a *deus ex machina*. What we are looking for is a slightly more reliable relation between the initial asymmetry and some built-in tendency towards its elimination or reduction. Perhaps such a relation can be made to arise out of the following conjecture, based primarily on the observation of United States-Latin American relations. A country whose trade or investment is dominated by ties to a large and rich country is, at some point, likely to devote its attention with single-minded concentration to this uncomfortable situation and to attempt to loosen or cut these ties. But the large rich country which carries on only a small portion of its international economic relations with the country it dominates is normally preoccupied with its more vital *other* interests, for example, with its relations to the other large powers. Hence our basic economic disparity generates a disparity of *attention*, or at least of high-level attention to use the language of bureaucratic politics, and this disparity now favors the *dependent* country: that country is likely to pursue its escape from domination more actively and energetically than the dominant country will work on preventing this escape. The British Empire is said to have been acquired in a fit of absent-mindedness. However that may be, it seems a more convincing proposition that empires, formal or informal, tend to crumble that way.

   In the United States, the lack of attention to Latin American affairs at the highest level of government has often been noted.[4] Generally it has been deplored; it leaves the field by default, so the argument goes, to the interests of those parties—traders, bankers, investors—with a direct, but narrow stake in these countries. Now it is quite correct that occasionally when, in some crisis, Latin American affairs were taken seriously at the highest level in Washington, it was perceived that the national interest of the United States by no means coincided with the short-term interests of individual trading or corporate groups, and actions were then taken that were more responsive than earlier low-level policies to the aspirations of Latin Americans. But it would be totally illegitimate to conclude from these few cases that Latin America would be bet-

---

[4] See in particular Richard Bloomfield, "Understanding United States Policy Toward Latin America: The Need for New Approaches," in A. F. Lowenthal and E. R. May, eds., *The United States and Latin America: The Politics of Policy-Making* (Harvard University Press, forthcoming).

ter off if its affairs were continually handled, like those of, say, China or Russia, at the highest levels of the United States government. From the point of view of Latin America's aspirations, the advantage of day-to-day policy being in the hands of lower-level diplomats heavily influenced by an intrusive business community is precisely that policies so formed are usually short-sighted as well as reasonably predictable. (Occasionally they become so inept and conflictual that they have to be corrected by a salvage operation staged at a higher level of policy making.) For these reasons they are no match for a determined adversary. In other words, if the efforts of a country to lessen its dependence are to prosper, there is no substitute for that "wise and salutary neglect" on the part of the imperial power which Burke long ago recognized as a basic cause of the growing strength of England's North American colonies. And it is my contention that the likelihood of such neglect—and of correspondingly concentrated attention on the part of the dependent country—is inscribed in the asymmetrical trade percentages just as much as the facts of dependence and domination themselves.

Insofar as US-Latin American relations are concerned, the preceding argument could be criticized by pointing to the numerous interventions of the United States in Latin American affairs, from the early ones in Mexico, the Caribbean, and Central America to the more recent actions in Guatemala, Cuba, the Dominican Republic, and Chile, to mention just the better known cases. What sort of neglect is it, one might well ask, that results in this pattern of conduct? It must be recognized that dominant power, be it the United States or the Soviet Union, has been able to bring military power to bear, overtly or covertly, when it judges that a country within its sphere of influence is breaking away or is otherwise going "too far." But this does not at all mean that the dependent country never has any room for maneuver. The point I have been making can be reformulated as follows: because of the disparity of attention dependent countries are in a favorable position to utilize what room for maneuver they have and may be able to widen this room; within limits that are often uncertain and constantly changing the dominant country is unlikely to pay the attention and make the effort needed to counter or effectively rein in dependent countries straining to achieve a greater degree of autonomy.

The possibility of a dialectical movement which would transform an asymmetrical relation, not into its opposite à la Hegel, but at least into a relation of considerably reduced asymmetry has been suggested here only for a specific variety of dependence—the one based on the sort of asymmetrical trading and investment pattern which was the focus of my book. There are actually a number of more familiar situations where initial domination or dependence activates tendencies in the opposite direction: for example, when a country which dominates the world market of one commodity or product raises its price and thereby eventually loses its monopoly because new producers elsewhere take advantage of the high supply price; or when a country that initially has little bargaining power in relation to a firm wishing to exploit its natural resources increases this power over time both because the firm's installations, once built, are captives of the country where they are located and because the country is likely, in due time, to insist on training its own technologists and other experts—a group that could run those installations in the event of takeover. In general, trade and investment relations between countries A and B may lead initially to dependence of B on A, for reason of the various asymmetries, but to the extent that economic intercourse increases the resources at B's command it becomes possible for B to pursue, by diversification and other means, a policy of lessening dependence, be it at the cost of some of these welfare gains.

It will be noted that the mechanisms through which such counterforces arise are very different from case to case: they range from purely economic reactions, as in the case of monopoly pricing, to purely political considerations, as in my attempt to show that an asymmetrical trading pattern will lead to asymmetrical degrees of attention to that pattern. To ferret out such mechanisms is anything but easy, particularly when, as in the latter case, initial asymmetry and dependency relations are grounded in economics while the countertendency relies on a certain kind of political reaction coming into play.

But the failure to discover the countertendencies is not due only to difficulties of crossing interdisciplinary boundaries; to a considerable extent it must be attributed to an intellectual orientation that is both undialectical and what I would call antipossibilist.[5] For many of the countertendencies that can be discovered are possibilities rather than certainties, and social scientists often consider it beneath their scientific dignity to deal with possibility until *after* it has become actual and can then at least be redefined as a probability.

These intellectual attitudes have affected much of the thinking on dependencia. Moreover, one of the main issues around which that thinking arose in the 1960s was the question whether the intensive industrialization Latin America had experienced since World War II was going to change radically its characteristics as a "periphery" that is dependent on a dominant "center." Dependencia theorists answered this question strongly in the negative and argued that an industrialized Latin America was, if anything, *more* dependent on the advanced countries than ever before, although in a different and perhaps more subtle manner. As happens frequently in the social sciences, the success of the theory rested in part on the nonobvious nature of its assertions; part of its success was also due to the naivete of those who had hailed industrialization as the cure-all of Latin America's poverty and backwardness. But the demonstration that hope for escape from domination is doomed over and over again, no matter what happens to the development of the productive forces, can hardly be repeated indefinitely. It would be reminiscent of the absurd Stalinist doctrine in the 1930s—which served of course to justify the purges—that the closer a country approaches the final stage of Communism the sharper the class struggle is bound to become and the more relentlessly it must be waged.

Fortunately some Latin American social scientists are recognizing that, in its original form, the dependencia thesis is subject to decreasing intellectual returns and have begun to explore the "contradictory character of social processes." As I hope to have shown here, these are the lines along which the more interesting discoveries are now to be made.

---

[5] See my advocacy of a "passion for the possible" (a phrase due to Kierkegaard) in the introduction to *A Bias for Hope: Essays on Development and Latin America* (New Haven, Conn.: Yale University Press, 1971), pp. 26–37.

Preface

Tᴴɪꜱ ᴇꜱꜱᴀʏ *was written in 1942 at the University of California, Berkeley, under a fellowship granted by the Rockefeller Foundation. It is an outgrowth of my collaboration with the Trade Regulation Project. Professor J. B. Condliffe directed this research project, and to him I owe my deepest gratitude, first, for enabling me to come from France to the United States in 1941, and, then, for giving me, after my arrival, the benefit of his advice and constant encouragement. I am also very greatly indebted to Professor Howard S. Ellis for his detailed criticism and numerous suggestions with respect to the content and form which this essay has taken. At successive stages of the work I was greatly helped by numerous discussions with my co-workers of the Trade Regulation Project, Dr. Alexander Gerschenkron, Dr. Peter Franck, and Mr. Alexander Stevenson. Mr. Stevenson is also responsible for many stylistic improvements. A trip to the Middle West and the East late in 1942 gave me an opportunity to place my manuscript before persons in a number of universities, and I wish to express my thanks to all those who took time to discuss my ideas with me. Finally, I am indebted to Dr. Fausto M. Ricci for calculating the indices and tables in Part 2. Chapter VII appeared in a slightly altered form, but under the same title, in the "Quarterly Journal of Economics," Volume LVII (August, 1943).*

Aʟʙᴇʀᴛ O. Hɪʀꜱᴄʜᴍᴀɴ

1945

Introduction

O<small>NLY</small> <small>THREE MONTHS</small> before he began work on *The Prince*, Machiavelli wrote in a letter to his friend and colleague, the Florentine diplomat Francesco Vettori: "Fortune has decreed that, as I do not know how to reason either about the art of silk or about the art of wool, either about profits or about losses, it befits me to reason about the state."[1] The Machiavellians of today would probably be astonished by this, since it reveals the complete failure of Machiavelli to perceive any connection between economics and politics.

A textbook for the modern prince should indeed contain, in addition to Machiavelli's classic chapters, extensive new sections on the most efficient use of quotas, exchange controls, capital investment, and other instruments of economic warfare. In this respect, practice has preceded theory. The extensive use of international economic relations as an instrument of national power policies has been, together with the "war of nerves," one of the main characteristics of the period preceding the outbreak of the present war.

Discussion of this development has not generally proceeded from a reëxamination of the various theories of imperialism. The proponents of these theories have tried to prove that the "inner contradictions of capitalism" lead inevitably to a struggle for markets and sources of raw materials. This struggle has been pictured as the main underlying cause of the bellicose policy of governments and of the ensuing wars. But present-day inquiries mostly take as possible or as given a power-minded policy, whatever may be its political, economic, or psychological origins, and examine the use which such a policy makes of the economic instruments at its disposal. Though not directly concerned with the "economic causes of war," this type of analysis can make clear important intermediate links in the process of causation of modern war.[2]

---

[1] "La fortuna ha fatto che non sapendo ragionare nè dell'arte della seta nè dell'arte della lana nè de'guadagni, nè delle perdite, e'mi conviene ragionare dello stato."— Letter of April 9, 1513, *in* Machiavelli, *Opere complete* (Florence, 1833), p. 856.
[2] See below, pp. 72 ff.

[xv]

What might be called the New Machiavellism has already received a good deal of attention. The German trade offensive and economic penetration in such areas as southeastern Europe and Latin America has been thoroughly investigated by many economists. The processes and technical devices by which Germany achieved partial or total success and the political, social, and economic circumstances which favored her during the 'thirties have been given careful study.

The present inquiry is directed to a more fundamental problem. It is concerned with the nature of a system of international trade that can very easily be exploited for purposes of national power policy. Is there in the trading system some inherent weakness which makes it vulnerable to the will of any government so minded to use it in the pursuit of power? Very little attention seems to have been given to this question. Yet its importance is obvious, since it points to an element in the international situation which is not necessarily temporary nor confined merely to the techniques and circumstances of which the Nazis took such good advantage. Upon the answer to this question may depend our position concerning the kind, extent, and organization of foreign trade which it will be desirable to reconstruct when the present war ends.

Our purpose is therefore to analyze the political aspect of international trade, the most important constituent of international economic relations. In this analysis we have found it useful to appeal to a variety of approaches—theoretical, historical, and statistical—which, it is hoped, will not blur the unity of our purpose.

We begin our study with a brief survey of economic thought on the relationship between foreign trade and national power, from the Mercantilists on. Chapter II attempts a systematic theoretical approach to the subject. It first makes clear the fundamental basis of the possible use of foreign trade as an instrument of national power policy. Using well-known concepts of economic analysis, it proceeds to show under what conditions and by means of what policies this instrument is likely to attain its highest efficiency. The principles of power policy thus deduced theoretically are then compared with the actual practices followed by German trading methods in recent years. Toward the end of this chapter the reader will be carried into a detailed discussion of certain problems of the theory of international trade which are touched upon earlier in the chapter.

Chapter III is applied to the historical background of our problem. It gives a survey of the literature on "economic aggression" before and during World War I and brings out the importance of the Paris Economic Conference of the Allies in 1916 for the Versailles Treaty and postwar economic policies. We shall see how opinion was divided in the main between two equally unsatisfactory positions: (1) the politicians, historians, and journalists, who, aided by protectionist economists, proposed to avert the danger of economic aggression by increased economic nationalism, and (2) the free trade economists who, answering on purely economic grounds, failed to see or denied the reality of the danger pointed out by their adversaries.

In the fourth chapter we review in the light of our theoretical and historical analyses certain safeguards or remedies which could be or have been proposed to prevent the use of foreign trade as an instrument of national power policies. We arrive at the conclusion that nothing short of a severe restriction of economic sovereignty can achieve this purpose effectively.

Certain questions raised in Part 1 can be answered in quantitative terms. Part 2 consists, therefore, of an exposition of various trends of international trade in recent years disclosed by statistical analysis.

We find that the total volume of trade handled by a country is an important factor in determining its power position in its dealings with any other single country. In Chapter V we therefore calculate an index number expressing the extent to which the trade of the large trading nations is or has been directed by preference toward the smaller trading countries.

The ability of a country to spread its imports and exports equally over a large number of countries affects in an important way its "economic independence." Since this point is especially important for the smaller countries, Chapter VI gives index numbers for the degree of concentration of their foreign trade on one or a few big markets or sources of supply.

Finally, in Chapter VII, we measure the extent to which world trade has been based primarily on an exchange of manufactures against raw materials and foodstuffs. We arrive at the result that the importance of this type of exchange has been much overrated relatively to other types: the exchange of (some) foodstuffs and raw materials against (some other) foodstuffs and raw materials, the exchange of (some) manufactures against (some other) manufactures, and the exchange of commodities in general against the so-called "invisible items" of the balances of payments. It is shown that the incorrect belief about the dominating position of the exchange of manufactures against foodstuffs and raw materials has led the old industrial countries, and in particular Germany, to fear the collapse of their foreign trade as a consequence of the industrialization of the agricultural countries. This fear contributes to the understanding of certain economic policies of Imperial as well as of Nazi Germany.[1]

Appendix A explains the statistical methods employed in Part Two. In this new edition, it should be reported that the index of concentration, which is proposed and discussed in that Appendix (pp. 157–162) and in Chapter VI, has become quite popular. The story of its diffusion, though, has been rather bizarre as can be gathered from the following complaint inserted by the author some years ago in the *American Economic Review* (I am happy to report that it has had some effect).

THE PATERNITY OF AN INDEX[2]

In the March issue of this *Review*, Benton F. Massell [5, pp. 52ff.] uses an index of trade concentration in the form $\sqrt{\Sigma(x_i/x)^2}$ where x_i is the value of a country's trade in commodity i (or with trading partner i) in some period, while x is the country's total trade. This index appears to have come into wide use recently and, to my rather chagrined surprise, is referred to, by Massell as well as by Kindleberger [4, p. 143], Michaeley [6], and Tinbergen [9, pp. 268ff.], as the "Gini index" or "Gini coefficient."[3] Given the sudden popularity of the measure, I feel that I should stand up for my rights as its originator. It was first introduced and computed for

---

[1] The following paragraphs have been added to the original text for the present edition.

[2] "The Paternity of an Index" originally appeared in *American Economic Review* 54 (September 1964), pp. 761–762.

[3] An honorable exception must be made for Coppock [1, pp. 97ff.].

a large number of countries in my book *National Power and the Structure of Foreign Trade* [3, Ch. 6 and pp. 157–162]. As explained there, the use of the index is indicated when concentration is a function of both unequal distribution *and fewness*. The traditional measures of concentration, generally devised in connection with income distribution and the Lorenz curve, are sensitive only to inequality of distribution, and we do owe several such measures to Gini.

The confusion on this score is the stranger as I referred at length in my book to the important work of the Italian statisticians on measurement of concentration, and particularly to Gini [3, pp. 157–158]. Upon devising the index I went carefully through the relevant literature because I strongly suspected that so simple a measure might already have occurred to someone. But no prior inventor was to be found.

To complicate the story, I must add that there was a posterior inventor, O. C. Herfindahl [2], who in 1950 proposed the same index, except for the square root. While obviously unaware of my earlier work when writing, Herfindahl did acknowledge it in a footnote [2, Ch. 1 and p. 21, n.]. Nevertheless, when the index is used for measuring industrial concentration, the second principal area of its application, it is now usually referred to as the "Herfindahl index," owing to a well-known paper by Rosenbluth [7] who has, however, recently made a valiant, but probably vain, attempt to straighten the matter out [8, pp. 391–392].

The net result is that my index is named either after Gini, who did not invent it at all, or after Herfindahl, who reinvented it. Well, it's a cruel world.

REFERENCES

1. Joseph D. Coppock, *International Economic Instability*. New York, 1962.
2. Orris C. Herfindahl, *Concentration in the U. S. Steel Industry*. Unpublished doctoral dissertation, Columbia University, 1950.
3. Albert O. Hirschman, *National Power and the Structure of Foreign Trade*. Berkeley 1945.

4. Charles P. Kindleberger, *Foreign Trade and the National Economy*. New Haven 1962.

5. Benton F. Massell, "Export Concentration and Fluctuations in Export Earnings," *American Economic Review*, March 1964, *54*, 47–63.

6. Michael Michaely, "Concentration of Exports and Imports: An International Comparison," *Economic Journal*, December 1958, *68*, 722–736.

7. Gideon Rosenbluth, "Measures of Concentration," in NBER *Business Concentration and Price Policy*, Princeton 1955, pp. 57–95.

8. ———, Remarks in *Die Konzentration in der Wirtschaft*, Schriften des Vereins für Sozialpolitik, New Series, Vol. 22, Berlin 1961, pp. 391–392.

9. Jan Tinbergen, *Shaping the World Economy*. New York 1962.

Contents

Part One

THEORETICAL AND HISTORICAL ASPECTS

CHAPTER I

Economic Thought on the Relationship Between Foreign Trade and National Power

BECAUSE OF an enduring liberal tradition, the conflict of social purposes which has been popularized by Goering's blunt statement of the choice to be made between guns and butter surprised great numbers of people in the democratic countries. Often-heard phrases, like the perversion of normal economic activities or the diversion of national wealth from its true economic purposes, indicate that in spite of the experience of the First World War the pursuit of power was still largely considered as a subordinate or exceptional aim of economic policy.

True it is that ever since Max Weber economists have had some doubts about the meaningfulness of the term economic when applied to ends and not to means. Nevertheless, academic discussion has sought mainly to determine which of the possible and sometimes conflicting definitions of welfare should be adopted as an objective of policy and what means would be most suitable to the kind of welfare desired.[1]

It is not surprising therefore that at first sight the pursuit of so different an objective as national power should have been deemed irreconcilable with the pursuit of any type of welfare. The alternative between guns and butter became, in academic language, the opposition between two economic systems, the economics of welfare and the economics of power.[2]

If the proposal to make the power of the state a primary aim of

---

[1] With respect to monetary policy, this self-imposed limitation of academic discussion has been pointed out recently by H. S. Ellis, "The Problem of Exchange Systems in the Post-War World," *The American Economic Review*, Supplement, Vol. XXXII (March, 1942), pp. 195–196.

[2] For a criticism of this terminology, see below, pp. 78 f.

economic policy was a shock to many contemporary minds, it never-theless formed the basis and even the *raison d'être* of earlier schools of economic thought, Machiavelli to the contrary notwithstanding. Perhaps Machiavelli's discounting of the connection between eco-nomics and politics might be explained by his desire to establish still better the complete autonomy of political science which he had separated so emphatically from its traditional metaphysical and ethical framework. But soon after him, writers on economic subjects were to point out the excellent use to which external and internal economic relations might be put by a state anxious to in-crease its power.

The policies advocated by the Mercantilists were to a large extent inspired by the double objective of increasing the wealth and the power of their own particular country. The reference by Bacon of a possible conflict between these two aims of economic policy seems to have been the one exception in a vast literature.[2] In general, the aim of increased national power at the expense of rival states, on the one hand, and the aim of increased wealth, on the other, were brought into complete harmony by the balance of trade doctrine, which led the Mercantilists to assume that in its external economic relations a nation can increase its wealth only by decreasing the wealth of other nations. The instrument of the shift was thought to be a balance of payments leading to an influx of gold and silver. An increase in the stock of precious metals would contribute indeed to the power of the state either directly by the accumulation of treas-ure or indirectly by enriching the country, which would thus be in a better position to contribute to the power of the state by taxes and services. The connection established by the Mercantilists be-tween wealth and national power may therefore be put in the form of a perfect syllogism:

Major premise: An increase of wealth of any country is an in-crease of its absolute power, and vice versa.

Minor premise: An increase of wealth of any country, if brought about by foreign trade, is necessarily a loss of wealth for other countries.

---

[2] Speaking of the Navigation Laws, Bacon said it was the "ancient policy of this estate" to bow "from considerations of plenty to considerations of power."—Quoted from Bacon's *History of the Reign of King Henry the Seventh*, in E. F. Heckscher, *Mercantilism*, Vol. II (London, 1935), p. 16. Cf. also the discussion on the place of

Conclusion: An increase of wealth through foreign trade leads to an increase of power relative to that of other countries—precisely the political aim of Mercantilist policy. Within the Mercantilist conception of wealth, a conflict between the wealth and power aims of the state is well-nigh unthinkable.

Adam Smith's best-known statement on our subject is, of course, that "defence is of much more importance than opulence."[4] If attention, however, is given only to this famous formula, his thought is easily seen in a false perspective. Before Smith, Hume had elaborately discussed in his *Essay on Commerce* the relationship between the "greatness of a state" and the "happiness of its subjects." He had reached the conclusion that "in the common course of human affairs" the two are in complete harmony, but he mentioned the possibility of exceptions to the rule.[5] Adam Smith's endorsement of "defence" in place of "opulence" is to be regarded as precisely such an exception. The Navigation Laws were indeed the only governmental interference with economic life in England to escape his criticism. In general, Adam Smith seems not to be concerned about the probability of a conflict between welfare and power. In one of his definitions of political economy, he states that "the great object of the political economy of every country is to increase the riches and the power of that country."[6] Although his emphasis with respect to these two aims is different from that of the Mercantilists, he declares expressly in his chapter on "The Expence of Defence": "In modern war the great expence of fire arms gives an evident advantage to the nation which can best afford this expence and consequently to an opulent and civilized over a poor and barbarous nation."[7] Thus, Adam Smith upheld the major premise of the Mercantilist syllogism even though wealth had not the same meaning for him as it had for the mercantilists.

It was the minor premise which crumbled under the weight of Adam Smith's proof that the gain of one nation is not necessarily the loss of another, but that, on the contrary, trade always benefits all participating nations. Therefore, the conclusion concerning the

power considerations in Mercantilist doctrines in Jacob Viner's review of Heckscher's work, in *Economic History Review*, Vol. II (1935), p. 100, and Heckscher's reply, *op. cit.*, Vol. VII (1936), p. 481.
    [4] Adam Smith, *Wealth of Nations*, Modern Library ed. (New York, 1937), p. 431.
    [5] David Hume, *Essays and Treatises on Several Subjects*, Vol. I (Edinburgh, 1800), pp. 271–282.   [6] Smith, *op. cit.*, p. 352.   [7] Smith, *op. cit.*, p. 669.

relative power of the country after the increase of wealth by foreign trade was no longer certain.[8]

This argument is at the root of the intellectual opposition of welfare and power which has been so well expressed by Mr. Hawtrey:

> So long as welfare is the end, different communities may coöperate happily together. Jealousy there may be and disputes as to how the material means of welfare should be shared. But there is no inherent divergence of aim in the pursuit of welfare. Power, on the other hand, is relative. The gain of one country is necessarily loss to others, its loss is gain to them. Conflict is the essence of the pursuit of power.[9]

Although the free trade argument is not logically conclusive from the point of view of a policy the main objective of which is *relative* power, it has not been exposed to much attack on this score. The main argument of the protectionists against free trade has long been directed to the supposed dangers inherent in excessive specialization. The inability under free trade conditions to develop national resources which would contribute to the economic and military power of the state and the apprehension of being cut off from essential supplies during an emergency have again and again proved two essential supports of protectionist and autarkic policy.

It would, of course, be a drastic oversimplification to view the conflict between protection and free trade as merely a struggle between the welfare and the power motives of commercial policy. If this were so, the antagonists in the field of foreign trade policy would have been talking entirely at cross-purposes. An examination of the reasons given for free trade or protection shows that both theories, never afraid of proving too much, have claimed:

1) that they are to be recommended on purely economic grounds;
2) that they lead to international peace;
3) that they are best fitted to prepare a country for war.

The numerous and often conflicting arguments advanced on either side made possible the charge of hypocrisy, with which the protectionists have been especially fond of taxing the free traders.

---

[8] Indeed, immediately after having proved that nations derive a mutual benefit from foreign trade, Adam Smith points to an instance in which welfare may be increased to the detriment of the power position of the country: "The wealth of a neighboring nation, however, though dangerous in war and politics, is certainly advantageous in trade."—Smith, *op cit.*, p. 461.

[9] R. G. Hawtrey, *The Economic Aspects of Sovereignty* (London, 1930), p. 27.

We are not concerned here with the economic arguments.[10] As to the noneconomic arguments for protectionism, it is historically interesting to note that they have not always been concerned with the conservation of certain social groups or with war preparedness. Lack of sympathy with foreign trade, because it might involve the nation in foreign entanglements, is a characteristic feature of American isolationism; an early and radical exponent of this idea was Fichte, who proposed his *Closed Commercial State* because he was convinced that commerce led inevitably to war. His ideal is a polyphonic humanity in which each nation, having closed its frontiers, achieves the full expression of its individuality.[11]

Among the noneconomic arguments for free trade, the main contention was of course that trade would prove a "bond of friendship between nations." When derided as utopians or accused of lack of patriotism, however, free traders have usually fallen back upon the argument that foreign trade enriches a country and thus helps its defense. This argument, which goes back to Adam Smith, has been repeated in defense of free trade ever since his day, especially in times of actual or impending war.[12] It is definitely linked with the somewhat outmoded theories stressing the *potentiel de guerre* as the main factor of war preparedness.

In addition, free traders have tried to belittle the danger of dependence pointed out by their adversaries. Thus, in the course of the Parliamentary Debates on the Corn Laws, Macaulay found an interesting counterargument to the charge of dependence arising out of free trade: "Next to independence, and indeed, amounting to practically the same thing," he argued, "is a very wide dependence, a dependence on the whole world, on every state and climate."[13]

The mention of climate is particularly revealing for the state of

---

[10] For a systematic analysis, see Gottfried Haberler, *The Theory of International Trade* (New York, 1937), pp. 221–295.

[11] J. G. Fichte, *Sämmtliche Werke,* Vol. III (Berlin, 1845), pp. 467–469, 483, 512.

[12] Cf. Ludwig V. Mises, "Vom Ziele der Handelspolitik," *Archiv für Sozialwissenschaft,* Vol. XLII (1916), p. 576; Lionel Robbins, "The Fundamental Reasons for Increased Protectionism," in *The Improvement of Commercial Relations Between Nations* (Paris, 1936), p. 27; also, Stefan Possony, *Tomorrow's War, Its Planning, Management and Cost* (London, 1938), pp. 147 f., 201; Wilhelm Röpke, *International Economic Disintegration* (London, 1942), pp. 101 f.

[13] Hansard (3d ser.), LX, 469, quoted in *Commerce and Industry,* ed. by William Page (London, 1919), p. 131. As we shall see later (on p. 73), the essence of this argument goes back to Adam Smith.

discussion which prevailed at that time—the advent of Great Britain's free trade policy. The connection between the potato famine in Ireland and the repeal of the Corn Laws in 1846 is well known. It was obvious that free trade, by extending the area of commerce, would lessen the dependence on weather and therefore the dangers of famine. This argument has been one of the main weapons of free traders ever since Adam Smith's discussion of the Corn Laws. Fichte felt the weight of the argument so much that in a special section of his *Closed Commercial State* he tried to show how, in the absence of foreign trade, the danger of famine could be obviated by the piling up of stocks in good years.[14] But for centuries wars and famines had been considered as two very similar and God-sent scourges of mankind. Only exceptional pessimists could imagine that a trend of development which pointed to the elimination of the danger of famine would not check, but would increase the dangers of war.[15]

It was, however, somewhat paradoxical to argue that the increased reliance of Great Britain on the outside world for her wheat supply would actually decrease her dependence in the event of war or of crop failure. Such an argument clearly presupposes either freedom of the seas or a mighty British fleet. Consequently, it has often been argued on the Continent that free trade was the "right" policy for England, but not for other countries. Macaulay's argument in favor of a greater geographical dispersion of commercial relations, however, has the great merit of pointing to the possibility of lessening the dependence created by foreign trade by modifying the distribution of that trade.

This idea could come to its full fruition only after commercial policy had been provided with the weapons necessary to influence the geographical distribution of foreign trade. As long as the most-favored-nation clause was prevalent in commercial treaties and trade was regulated mostly by tariffs, governments had relatively little influence upon the geographical course of trade, or, at any rate, were not fully conscious of possessing this influence. In the

[14] Fichte, *op. cit.*, pp. 428–431. How, in a world of surpluses, this argument has fallen into oblivion has been pointed out recently by Röpke, *op. cit.*, p. 143.

[15] An example of this kind of pessimism is given by a passage of Flaubert's correspondence: "The great collective (public) works, like the construction of the Suez Canal, might well be, in another form, adumbrations and preparations of these monstrous conflicts which we cannot conceive!"—*Correspondance*, Vol. IV (Paris, 1893), p. 29.

interest of their power policy, they tried to strike a rough balance between the economic and possible military advantages of foreign trade on the one side and its dangers on the other.

This is the policy actually advocated in a study by Herbert Wergo, a German economist writing before the advent of Hitler on the alternative virtues of free trade and protectionism in promoting the power policy of the state.[16] According to Wergo, free trade and protectionism should not be considered as mutually exclusive policies. Both can be of service to the state. The practical outcome of such a theory would be the division of the national economy into two parts, a protected one, considered as "essential," and a free part, the aim of which would be to secure a cheap and plentiful supply of "nonessential" goods. Actually, this was the policy pursued by most states even before the outbreak of the First World War.

All these policies proposed by free traders, protectionists, or eclectics as being conducive to more *economic* power have the common characteristic that they do not necessarily lead to an increase in *relative* power, which is, after all, the only objective that matters. It is true that the danger of a nation's falling behind other nations because of the lack of a proper policy was often pointed out. But if all nations pursued the "right" policy—whatever this was held to be—protectionists and free traders alike could have no reasonable hope of a change in the balance of economic power in favor of any particular country. In other words, the contribution of commercial policy to the power of the state was thought of more as a necessary condition for the successful forging of the weapons than as one of the weapons making power supremacy possible.

This position was a natural one for the free traders whose whole case rested on the demonstration of the mutual benefit accruing from commercial intercourse to the various countries trading together. But the protectionists had their eyes fixed exclusively upon the dependence incurred through foreign trade by their respective national economies. Thus, they overlooked the fact that the dependence created by trade, like the benefit derived from it, has a double aspect.[17]

---

[16] Herbert Wergo, *Freihandel und Schutzzoll als Mittel staatlicher Machtentfaltung*, Probleme der Weltwirtschaft, Vol. 45 (Jena, 1928).

[17] In international investments exactly the opposite neglect has been prevalent, i.e., only the influence acquired through investments in other countries has generally been

This double aspect—the fact that dependence of country A on country B implies at the same time dependence of B on A—had on the contrary been seized upon by the internationalists who saw in it the basis for their hope that trade would create national or at least strong sectional interests opposed to war.[18] To convey this idea they used the terms mutual dependence, interdependence, inextricable network of markets, etc. This line of thought has a long history which can be traced back to Montesquieu.[19] Its best-known exponents are Cobden and Sir Norman Angell, although the latter's outlook is far less optimistic than that of Cobden, because Sir Norman no longer takes it for granted that man will always eventually perceive and follow his real interests.

In his famous eulogy of international trade, John Stuart Mill adhered to the view that commerce caused mutual dependence and would thereby constitute a force for peace.[20] But by his contributions to economic theory he undermined at the same time these very hopes. The necessary basis for the idea that the interdependence created by trade would or should lead to a peaceful collaboration between nations, is, indeed, the belief that the dependence of A on B is roughly the same as the dependence of B on A. Mill was one of the first to show that the material benefit derived from international trade is not necessarily divided equally between the various trading nations.[21] Ever since Mill's time Anglo-Saxon economists

---

given consideration. Staley has pointed out that by investing abroad a nation also becomes more or less dependent upon the country in which it invests. He writes: "Objectively, one can think of respects in which American policy becomes subject to influences from Europe as a result of capital investments in Europe, as well as of ways in which European policy becomes subject to influences from America—in fact in the realm of foreign policy and as between advanced countries, there is strong reason for believing that the borrowing nation has more leverage on the policies of the creditor nation than vice versa."—Eugene Staley, *War and the Private Investor* (New York, 1935), p. 406.

[18] This argument is distinct from, though related to, the idea that commerce, bringing about the very enrichment which is the aim or pretext of most wars, would render war *unnecessary*. (See below, pp. 28 f.)

[19] "The natural effect of commerce is to bring about peace. Two nations which trade together, render themselves reciprocally dependent: if the one has an interest in buying the other has an interest in selling; and all unions are based upon mutual needs."—Montesquieu, *De l'Esprit des Lois*, Book XX, Chap. II, in *Œuvres*, Vol. I (Amsterdam and Leipzig), p. 446.

[20] "It is commerce which is rapidly rendering war obsolete, by strengthening and multiplying the personal interests which are in natural opposition to it."—John Stuart Mill, *Principles of Political Economy*, 7th ed. (London, 1929), p. 582.

[21] J. S. Mill, *Essays on Some Unsettled Questions of Political Economy*, Essay I (London, 1844), pp. 1–46.

have given much thought to the ways in which the terms of trade might be altered by changing conditions or by adopting policies favorable to one nation. Bastable later showed how, under the hypothesis of trade between two socialist states, the theory of bilateral monopoly would become applicable.[22] The country with superior bargaining power might, on this basis, be able to obtain the whole gain from trade. Similar situations were found to prevail when trade takes place between two countries of different size or with different degrees of specialization.[23] Preoccupation with questions of this type has even led Edgeworth to affirm that "the principal characteristic peculiar to international trade is, I think, the possibility of a nation benefiting itself by a tax on exports and imports."[24]

Thus, although the reasoning of the Mercantilist balance of trade theory had been decisively discredited by the criticism of Hume and Adam Smith, some of its main conclusions were rehabilitated, not as a certainty, but as a possibility by the theory of the terms of trade: It was shown that international trade might work to the exclusive or disproportionate benefit of one or a few of the trading nations.

It need not surprise us that the obvious power implications of these findings for the political dependence arising from trade, somewhat neglected by English economists, have been seized upon by their German colleagues. Thus, Max Sering wrote as early as 1900: "It has been wrongly contended that in the economic intercourse of nations the dependence is always a mutual one, that always equal values are exchanged. As between private persons, there exist between national economies relations of exploitation and of subjection."[25] But Sering, engaged in giving plausible reasons for the building of a German fleet, did not pay much attention to the economic conditions and techniques which would lead to such an unequal distribution of the mutual dependence arising from trade.

[22] C. F. Bastable, *The Theory of International Trade*, 4th ed. (London, 1903), pp. 25–29; see also criticism by F. Y. Edgeworth, "The Theory of International Values," *Economic Journal*, Vol. IV (1894), p. 622.

[23] Cf. J. S. Nicholson, *Principles of Political Economy* (London, 1897), pp. 309–311; see also Haberler, *op. cit.*, pp. 148–149.

[24] F. Y. Edgeworth, *Papers Relating to Political Economy*, Vol. II (London, 1925), p. 19.

[25] Max Sering, "Die Handelspolitik der Grossmächte und die Kriegsflotte," in *Handels- und Machtpolitik*, Vol. II (Stuttgart, 1900), p. 31.

Only scattered thoughts on this subject can be found in the subsequent literature. We shall attempt here a systematic exposition of the question of why and how foreign trade might become or might consciously and efficiently be used as an instrument of national power policy. The main contributions in this field have been practical ones, the German trade offensive in southeastern Europe being the outstanding and most recent example. We believe that by a theoretical analysis we may arrive at a fundamental diagnosis and ultimate cure of the ills which under the names of "economic penetration" and "bloodless invasion" have repeatedly afflicted recent history.

CHAPTER II

Foreign Trade As an Instrument of National Power

IN THIS WORK the term *national power* is used in the sense of power of coercion which one nation may bring to bear upon other nations, the method of coercion being military or "peaceful." In trying to expand its power a nation must take account of many factors—historical, political, military, psychological, and economic. Among the economic determinants of power, foreign trade plays an important part. In order to analyze the way in which foreign trade contributes to a certain distribution of power among the various nations, it must be isolated temporarily from the other determinants; for the purpose of our inquiry these other determinants may be impounded in a vast *ceteris paribus* upon which, for the sake of rendering our analysis more realistic, we shall have to draw from time to time.

It will then be our aim to understand why and how relationships of dependence, of influence, and even of domination can arise out of trade relations. We are not concerned with the opposite line of causation which also exists and which may even have had a greater historical importance: the question of how a given distribution of power influences trade relations. It will, however, be well for the reader to remember that frequently the adoption of certain economic policies leading to greater power for a given nation is possible only if there exists an initial power disequilibrium in favor of that nation.

Colonial trade often gives us the opportunity of observing this type of cumulative effect. An initial power supremacy enables the imperial power to shape the direction and composition of the colony's trade, and the trade relations which are thus established in turn strengthen markedly the original power position held by the imperial power.

THE TWO EFFECTS OF FOREIGN TRADE

Foreign trade has two main effects upon the power position of a country. The first effect is certain to be positive: By providing a more plentiful supply of goods or by replacing goods wanted less by goods wanted more (from the power standpoint), foreign trade enhances the potential military force of a country. This we may call the *supply effect* of foreign trade. It not only serves to strengthen the war machine of a country, but it uses the threat of war as a weapon of diplomacy. Although we have seen that free traders have advised statesmen to rely on the supply effect of foreign trade, protectionists have warned them of the dangers of its cessation during war, which, they say, is precisely when it will be most needed. But this danger might be lessened and the supply effect safeguarded:

1) by securing control of the oceanic trade routes;
2) by a policy of extensive preventive accumulation of stock piles in times of peace;
3) by redirecting trade toward those countries from which the danger of being cut off is minimized.

The attempt to trade more with neighboring, friendly, or subject countries is largely inspired by this consideration, and it has been one of the most powerful motive forces behind the policies of regionalism and empire trade.

All these points are obvious and hardly need further elaboration. As far as the supply effect is concerned, foreign trade serves as a means of increasing the efficiency of the military pressure which one country might bring to bear upon other countries. But, just as war or the threat of war can be considered in turn as a means of obtaining a certain result, so the supply effect of foreign trade is an indirect instrument of power, the direct instrument being war or the threat of war. In its final result, therefore, the supply effect of foreign trade requires at least the possibility of war.

The second effect of foreign trade from the power standpoint is that it may become a direct source of power. It has often been hopefully pointed out that commerce, considered as a means of obtaining a share in the wealth of another country, can supersede war.[1] But

---

[1] This idea, which points to trade as an "economic equivalent to war," appears, for example, in the following characteristic passage from the famous anti-Napoleon tract

commerce can become an alternative to war also—and this leads to a less optimistic outlook—by providing a method of coercion of its own in the relations between sovereign nations. Economic warfare can take the place of bombardments, economic pressure that of saber rattling. It can indeed be shown that even if war could be eliminated, foreign trade would lead to relationships of dependence and influence between nations. Let us call this the *influence effect* of foreign trade, and, because of its importance, give the greater part of this chapter to its analysis.

The terms dependence and influence have hitherto been used indiscriminately to describe the situation which seems invariably to arise out of the trade relations between two sovereign states. But why does such a situation arise at all? In other words, what is the root cause of the political or power aspect of international economic relations? To answer this question we must concede that the explanation of the great power held in the past by Great Britain was the fact that she possessed strategic bases, such as Gibraltar, Suez, and Singapore. The possession of these bases had two consequences: First, it guaranteed the security of British trade; second, as a welcome by-product, it enabled Great Britain to cut off the trade of other countries passing through these points, be it trade with Great Britain or trade between two other countries. This second consequence gave her considerable direct power over, and influence in, other countries, in that they were always exposed to the potential threat of a sudden stoppage of their trade at Britain's will.

But every sovereign nation has some influence of this kind, since through the control of its frontiers and the power over its citizens it can at any time interrupt *its own export and import trade,* which is at the same time the import and export trade of some other countries. The stoppage of this trade obliges the other countries to find

<hr />

of Benjamin Constant: "War and commerce are but two different means of arriving at the same aim which is to possess what is desired. Trade is nothing but a homage paid to the strength of the possessor by him who aspires to the possession; it is an attempt to obtain by mutual agreement that which one does not hope any longer to obtain by violence. The idea of commerce would never occur to a man who would always be the strongest. It is experience, proving to him that war, i.e., the use of his force against the force of others, is exposed to various resistances and various failures, which makes him have recourse to commerce, that is, to a means more subtle and better fitted to induce the interest of others to consent to what is his own interest."—*De l'Esprit de Conquête et de l'Usurpation dans leurs rapports avec la Civilisation Européenne,* Part I, Chap. II.

alternative markets and sources of supply and, should this prove impossible, it forces upon them economic adjustments and lasting impoverishment. True, the stoppage of trade will also do harm to the economy of the country taking the initiative in bringing about the stoppage, but this is not unlike the harm an aggressive country can do to itself in making war on another. A country trying to make the most out of its strategic position with respect to its own trade will try precisely to create conditions which make the interruption of trade of much graver concern to its trading partners than to itself. Tariff wars and interruptions of trade rarely occur, but the awareness of their possibility is sufficient to test the influence of the stronger country and to shape the policy of the weaker.

That economic pressure upon a country consists mainly of the threat of severance and ultimately of actual interruption of external economic relations with that country was clearly recognized by Article 16 of the Covenant of the League of Nations. The intention of Article 16 was to coördinate and combine the power positions which the various member states of the League had acquired in the aggressor country by entertaining commercial and financial relations with it.

Thus, the power to interrupt commercial or financial relations with any country, considered as an attribute of national sovereignty, is the root cause of the influence or power position which a country acquires in other countries, just as it is the root cause of the "dependence on trade." It should be noted that the only condition for the emergence of these political aspects of trade relations is that of unfettered national sovereignties. It has often been pointed out that central regulation by separate sovereign units leads to a dangerous "politicalization" of trade.[2] Undoubtedly the identification of every private interest with national interest and prestige may add a heavy strain on international relations. But state regulation by no means *creates* the political aspects of international economic relations (as the term politicalization seems to imply). It merely emphasizes them or makes them more apparent and exploitable. For the political or power implications of trade to exist and to make them-

---

[2] J. B. Condliffe, *The Reconstruction of World Trade* (New York, 1940), p. 56; Lionel Robbins, *Economic Planning and International Order* (London, 1937), pp. 90 f.; Sir Arthur Salter, "The Future of Economic Nationalism," *Foreign Affairs*, Vol. X (October, 1932), p. 18; Eugene Staley, *World Economy in Transition* (New York, 1939), p. 178.

selves felt, it is not essential that the state should exercise positive action, i.e., organize and direct trade centrally; the negative right of veto on trade with which *every* sovereign state is invested is quite sufficient.[3] We shall now examine the conditions making this right of veto or the power to interrupt trade an effective weapon in the struggle for power. To bring these conditions about will obviously be the goal of a nation using foreign trade as an instrument of power policy.[4]

THE INFLUENCE EFFECT OF FOREIGN TRADE (SECTION 1)

What we have called the influence effect of foreign trade derives from the fact that the trade conducted between country A, on the one hand, and countries B, C, D, etc., on the other, is worth *something* to B, C, D, etc., and that they would therefore consent to grant A certain advantages—military, political, economic—in order to retain the possibility of trading with A. If A wants to increase its hold on B, C, D, etc., it must create a situation in which these countries would do *anything* in order to retain their foreign trade with A. Such a situation arises when it is extremely difficult and onerous for these countries:

    1) to dispense entirely with the trade they conduct with A, or
    2) to replace A as a market and a source of supply with other countries.

The principles of a power policy relying on the influence effect of foreign trade are in their essence extremely simple: *They are all designed to bring about this "ideal" situation.*

---

[3] The powers of the state with respect to foreign trade conducted by private enterprise may be compared to the powers of a labor union which, though refraining from collective bargaining, would have the power to call a strike and to determine its length. It will probably be granted that, in this case, most of the effects of combination would still obtain.

[4] Since the power position of a country will be of importance in its commercial negotiations, the inquiry which follows gives incidentally an analysis of what is commonly called bargaining power. This term, however, for three distinct reasons, is inadequate for our purposes. First, the achieving of tariff and similar concessions is only one of the many uses to which the political power arising from foreign trade might be put; cf., in this connection, Hans Staudinger, "The Future of Totalitarian Barter Trade," *Social Research,* Vol. VII (November, 1940), p. 426. In the second place, bargaining power in commercial negotiations is traditionally associated with a certain position of the trade balance between the two countries in negotiation, a view which will be explained and criticized below (pp. 32 f.). Third, the term bargaining power has a definite meaning in the theory of bilateral monopoly which is markedly different from the meaning which it would assume in our analysis. This difference and its implications are shown on pages 45–46 of this chapter.

Our analysis of these principles is divided into two parts. In the first, it is assumed that the countries which are the objects of the power policy have no possibility of shifting their trade with A to each other or to third countries, whereas country A remains free to trade with whatever country it desires. Given this assumption, which will be dropped in the second part of our analysis, we have to pay attention only to the first characteristic of the "ideal" situation.

The difficulty for country B, C, D, etc., of dispensing with the trade conducted with A seems to depend on three main factors:

1) The total net gain to B, C, D, etc., of their trade with A;
2) The length and the painfulness of the adjustment process which A may impose upon B, C, D, etc., by interrupting trade;
3) The strength of the vested interests which A has created by its trade within the economies of B, C, D, etc.

GAIN FROM TRADE AND DEPENDENCE ON TRADE

The influence which country A acquires in country B by foreign trade depends in the first place upon the total gain which B derives from that trade; the total gain from trade for any country is indeed nothing but another expression for the total impoverishment which would be inflicted upon it by a stoppage of trade. In this sense the classical concept, gain from trade, and the power concept, dependence on trade, now being studied are seen to be merely two aspects of the same phenomenon, and this connection can serve as a modern application of the ancient saying *fortuna est servitus*.

The whole theory of the gain from trade and its distribution therefore becomes relevant to our subject. The gain from trade has been defined by Marshall in the following terms: "The direct gain which a country derives from her foreign trade is the excess of the value to her of the things which she imports over the value to her of the things which she could have made for herself with the capital and labour devoted to producing the things which she exported in exchange for them."[5] This definition brings out clearly that the gain from trade cannot be measured either by comparing the satisfaction derived from the consumption of the imports with the satisfaction which could be derived from the consumption at home of the exports or by comparing the hypothetical domestic cost of the imported com-

---

[5] Alfred Marshall, *Money, Credit and Commerce* (London, 1923), pp. 109–110.

modities with their actual cost.[6] If a country was shut off from trade
it would normally neither continue to produce the goods formerly
exported nor try to produce at home all the goods formerly imported, but, given the reduced resources, an adjustment would take
place toward the production of the goods most desired.

Professor Viner has elaborated an even more complex concept
of the gain from trade. He has shown that differences in satisfaction
between the trade and the no-trade situation might occur not only
through a different composition of the goods to be consumed in the
two situations, but also because of differences in the occupational
pattern or in the general balance between work and leisure in the
country concerned.[7]

Provided we keep in mind the qualification arising from these
considerations, Marshall's definition still gives a good account of
the value of trade to a country or, in other words, of that part of a
country's well-being which it is in the power of its trading partners
to take away.

The first conclusion which could be drawn from the connection
which we have established between gain from trade and dependence
on trade is that in order to increase its influence in other nations,
nation A should simply bring about an expansion of its foreign
trade. In accordance with a general presumption established by
theory, a voluntary increase of trade on the part of A's trading partners is indeed indicative of an increase of their gains from trade
and, hence, of their dependence on A. But this reasoning overlooks
the fact that in this way the influence which the other nations hold
in country A would also be increased. Some countries might be able
to neglect this consideration because of their geographical position,
their military power, or other noneconomic elements. But, in general, a country embarking on a power policy will have fixed for the
amount of its trade relations with foreign countries a certain maximum limit which it will think unsafe to exceed.[8]

---

[6] The latter error was attributed by Malthus to Ricardo. Cf. Jacob Viner, *Studies in the Theory of International Trade* (New York, 1937), p. 528.

[7] Viner, *op. cit.*, pp. 519 ff.

[8] It remains true that complete autarky can hardly be considered as an element of an intelligent power policy. And if the nations which have proclaimed autarky as their ultimate goal have remained far off the mark, this may be due not only to the economic difficulties which they have experienced in trying to dispense with foreign trade, but also because they have found it politically inexpedient to do without trade relations.

If we take account of this objection, another method might be proposed: country A, seeking to increase its influence in country B, might have an interest in altering the terms of trade in B's favor. Here, then, it would seem, we have an ideal instance of the opposition between a policy trying to maximize national income and a policy setting out to maximize national power.

This statement, however, needs qualification and elaboration. In the first place, the functional relationship between gain from trade and dependence on trade points to a potential clash, not only between national income or welfare and power, but also between the two different types of power policy, the one relying mostly on the supply effect of foreign trade and the other relying upon the influence effect. It is indeed clear that a policy using foreign trade as its instrument may sometimes have to choose between better terms of trade, i.e., more plentiful supply of needed materials for a given quantity of home products, on the one hand, and more influence on the trading partner, on the other.

But is there an inevitable conflict between national welfare and national power, or, within a power policy, between the supply effect and the influence effect of foreign trade? This is a necessary conclusion only if we accept the common conception that a given amount of trade results in a fixed total gain to be distributed between the trading countries according to some ratio determined by the terms of trade. An increase of the gain of A can then only be procured at the cost of a decrease of the gain of B. This view, however, should be suspect if only because of its resemblance to the cruder Mercantilist idea that A's gain is B's loss.

Actually we have here to clear up a terminological confusion which is at the root of the whole matter. What is commonly called total gain from trade is by no means, as one might expect, the sum of the gains from trade as defined by Marshall for the individual participating countries. The term total gain, as used generally, is rather to be understood as the physical surplus of goods made possible by the international division of labor. This physical surplus is indeed fixed under given cost and demand conditions. It might be called the total objective gain from trade. But a moment's reflection should show that although this objective gain might be wholly nonexistent (as in the absence of any international specialization following the opening up of trade), a substantial *subjective* gain as defined by Marshall might still accrue to the various countries, provided only that they do not produce the same range of commodities.[9]

If, therefore, an objective gain from trade in the form of a physical surplus of goods is not even a necessary condition for the emergence of a subjective gain from trade, the existence of a close relationship between the distribution of the objective and the subjective gains as between the countries trading together may be legitimately doubted. The theory of the terms of trade has succeeded in showing how the objective gain is distributed and how its distribution can be affected by changes in tastes and techniques or by commercial policies. It has generally been thought that the terms of trade give a broad indication of the gain from trade; and in spite of its many limitations pointed out by Professor Viner,[10] this method of approach still seems fruitful if one is interested mainly in knowing when a country increases or decreases the gain from its trade with another specified country, as this can under static conditions—i.e., with tastes and techniques constant—occur only through a movement of the terms of trade in its favor. But the method fails us decisively if we are interested, not in the increments of the subjective gain from trade, but in its total amount for any given situation. It is indeed not possible to assert that the respective extents of the subjective gains from trade correspond to the division of the objective gain without assuming for the two countries a similarity of tastes and of the levels of satisfaction prior to trade—in other words, without assuming the whole problem away. In the absence of such assumptions there is no reason whatsoever why a country should not obtain a smaller part of the physical surplus of goods obtained by international specialization whilst deriving a larger increase in satisfaction from trade than its trading partner.[11]

---

[9] Even under the very simplest classical assumptions of two commodities of similar importance, two countries of similar size, constant costs, absence of transport costs, and similar tastes in the two countries, it can be shown that further specialization after the opening up of trade, as required by the principle of comparative cost, is not a prerequisite for the existence of some subjective increase in satisfaction from trade. Cf. diagrammatical exposition of this case on pages 49–52 of this chapter.

[10] Viner, *op. cit.*, pp. 555–582.

[11] The belief that the position of the terms of trade gives a clue to the respective extent of the subjective gains from trade has been much strengthened by the often-quoted case of two countries of unequal size trading in two commodities. In this hypothesis the larger country specializes only partly, its pre-trade ratio of exchange

The inquiry into the factors which determine the amount of the subjective gain from trade has to be made directly. It has been undertaken with the help of diagrammatical illustrations by the neoclassical writers, Edgeworth[12] and, in particular, Marshall.[13] Marshall's conclusion, which is unaffected by two errors in his method,[14] is that "the surplus (of country G) is the greater, the more urgent is G's demand for a small amount of E's goods and the more of them she can receive without any great movement of the rate of interchange in her favor." In other words, with a given volume of trade the subjective gain is smallest if the supply-demand schedule of a country maintains a high elasticity throughout its relevant part; whereas the gain would be largest if a country's demand, after having been very elastic for small amounts of the other country's goods, becomes inelastic in its later (and relevant) stages.[15]

---

between the two commodities remains unchanged and the whole physical surplus of production due to specialization accrues to the smaller country whilst the supply in goods of the larger country remains unchanged. But so far from being an illustration of the general correspondence between the position of the terms of trade and the extent of the subjective gains, this is actually the only case in which the correspondence holds—a quite paradoxical case—as trade leads neither to an increase in quantity nor to a change in composition of the goods consumed in one of the trading countries.

[12] F. Y. Edgeworth, "On the Application of Mathematics to Political Economy," *Journal of the Royal Statistical Society*, Vol. LII (1889), pp. 558–560. Edgeworth reproduces in the main the "beautiful reasoning" of Auspitz and Lieben, *Untersuchungen über die Theorie der Preise* (Leipzig, 1889), pp. 413–415. In a later work, "The Theory of International Values," *Economic Journal*, Vol. IV (1894), Edgeworth deals essentially with the increments in the gain from trade, not with the total amount; cf. Viner, *op. cit.*, p. 576 and footnote 3.

[13] Marshall, *op. cit.*, Appendix J, pp. 338–340.

[14] As pointed out with respect to the algebraic illustration by Allyn A. Young, "Marshall on Consumer's Surplus in International Trade," *Quarterly Journal of Economics*, Vol. XXXIX (1924), pp. 144–150, and with respect to the diagrammatical exposition by Viner, *op. cit.*, pp. 570–575. Viner also shows that the more general objection of Allyn A. Young against the whole concept of Marshall's "surplus" in international trade (which is nothing but another expression for the subjective gain from trade) does not hold.

[15] In this context elasticity means the response of the imported quantity to a change in the terms of trade. Although it is not identical with the ordinary concept of demand elasticity, it is related to it. Cf. T. O. Yntema, *A Mathematical Reformulation of the General Theory of International Trade* (Chicago, 1932), pp. 52–56. Professor Kindleberger has shown the inconsistent use made by various economists of the term urgent demand and has proposed the terms flexible and inflexible demand instead of not urgent and urgent demand; cf. C. P. Kindleberger, "Flexibility of Demand in International Trade Theory," *Quarterly Journal of Economics*, Vol. LI (February, 1937), pp. 352–361. He, however, as our quotation shows, is incorrect in contending that Marshall did not use the term urgent demand; paying attention only to the ordinary Marshallian price elasticity, Professor Kindleberger does not realize that Marshall's elasticity concepts, as developed in connection with his foreign trade curves, can take care of the various situ-

This statement may seem surprising, as a country which finds itself in the latter situation is generally said to be in an inferior strategic position and to be exposed to a manipulation of the terms of trade against it. Actually, however, this is only another aspect of the same situation: A country which gains much from the exchange of its home produce against imports may be maneuvered more easily into concessions according to the rate of interchange than a country for which trade is only barely profitable under existing conditions.

We have mentioned above the possibility that a country, though obtaining a smaller objective gain from trade, may still enjoy a greater subjective gain; it is now seen that this situation is not necessarily an oddity, but may, on the contrary, be considered as probably true.[10]

These theoretical considerations are directly relevant to the twofold object of a power policy by foreign trade which we have described. Country A may possibly increase the gain from trade and therefore the dependence of its trading partners either by a change

---

ations which arise in international trade and are denoted by the terms urgent or inflexible. It remains true that these special terms are useful in shortening the description of the shape of a Marshallian demand-supply curve which is at first extremely responsive to favorable changes in the terms of trade and becomes inelastic for further changes in these terms. The conflicting interpretations of the term urgent demand derive from the fact that the various writers have considered different stretches of the *same* supply-demand curve. Professor Kindleberger rightly shows the connection between the concept of urgency of demand and that of income elasticity. The two, however, are not identical, since income elasticity means responsiveness of the demand of a commodity to income increases, whereas the elasticity of the Marshallian curve means responsiveness of demand of a commodity to a favorable change of its rate of exchange for another commodity.

[10] It seems that J. S. Mill had this situation in mind when he wrote in his *Essays on Some Unsettled Questions:* "If the question be now asked, which of the countries of the world gains most by foreign commerce, the following will be the answer. If by gain be meant advantage, in the most enlarged sense, that country will generally gain the most, which stands most in need of foreign commodities. But if by gain be meant saving of labor and capital in obtaining the commodities which the country desires to have, whatever they may be; the country will gain, not in proportion to its own need of foreign articles, but to the need which foreigners have of the articles which itself produces."—J. S. Mill, *op. cit.,* p. 44; cf. also p. 46. Mill has not reproduced this passage in the *Principles* where he has elaborated only the second concept of gain; indeed, the first one hardly fits in with his value theory. Jevons obviously ignored Mill's earlier writings when, as exposed in the *Principles,* he attacked the concept of gain in the following terms: "So far is Mill's statement (about the distribution of the gain from trade) from being fundamentally correct that I believe the truth lies in the opposite direction. As a general rule, the greatness of the price which a country is willing and able to pay for the production of other countries measures or at least manifests, the greatness of the benefit which it derives from such imports."—Stanley Jevons, *The Theory of Political Economy,* 4th ed. (London, 1911), p. 145.

in the composition of trade or by a change in partners without having to submit to more unfavorable terms of trade. To resolve in this way the conflict between the supply effect and the influence effect of foreign trade which at first seemed inevitable, A has to seek trading partners with an "urgent" demand for its export goods.

In the first place, A will therefore turn to countries which have no possibilities of themselves producing the commodities country A exports. A second and more general case, which has been pointed out by Marshall, is the trade with "poor countries," that is, countries with low real incomes before the opening up of trade. Marshall has applied to this case the "law of the diminishing marginal utility of income" in the following terms: "The rich country can with little effort supply a poor country with implements for agriculture or the chase which doubled the effectiveness of her labor, and which she could not make for herself; while the rich country could without great trouble make for herself most of the things which she purchased from the poor nation or at all events could get fairly good substitutes for them. A stoppage of the trade would therefore generally cause much more real loss to the poor than to the rich nation."[17]

A nation pursuing a power policy may be assumed to export industrial goods and to import mainly those articles for which it has either no substitutes at home or only poor and expensive ones. It must be prepared to incur a certain dependence on foreign countries in order to obtain these articles—or, in our terminology, in order to profit from the supply effect of foreign trade. Its problem is there-

---

[17] Marshall, *op. cit.*, p. 168. It will be noted that, for Marshall, the case of a rich country trading with a poor country and the case of a country having a monopoly in some article trading with another country having no such monopoly are somewhat intertwined. A conclusion similar to that of Marshall follows from Edgeworth's comment on his own assumption in the analysis of foreign trade that "the hedonic worth of money is the same in both countries"; he conceded indeed that "when we know that one party is much better off than another, the assumption may be illegitimate."— "The Theory of International Values," *Economic Journal*, Vol. IV (1894), p. 436. That the comparison of utilities between two collective groups, such as countries, is less rather than more hazardous than intrapersonal comparisons of utility has been shown by a recent contribution (L. G. Melville, "Economic Welfare," *Economic Journal*, Vol. XLIX [September, 1939], pp. 552–553). The possible exceptions to the case which have been pointed out by Marshall are not likely to arise from the difference in the "capacity for enjoyment" of the citizens of the two countries, but rather from the difference in the effect of foreign trade upon the distribution of income in the two countries. If, indeed, the goods imported into the relatively poor country add mainly to the enjoyment of its wealthier classes, whereas the contrary happens in the relatively rich country, the effect described by Marshall may well be neutralized.—I am indebted to Dr. Fellner for this point.

fore how to induce a maximum dependence of foreign countries, given a fixed dependence of its own. In solving this problem it can avail itself of our findings by determining what to export and by choosing the countries from which to import.[18] It can see to it, first, that it possesses a monopolistic position in its export articles by directing trade to those countries which are relatively poorly suited to produce these or similar articles. In our case this means the agricultural countries; and the prevention of industrialization or even the removal of already existing industries is an important part of a policy of trying to preserve or to increase the influence acquired in these countries by an industrial nation.

In the second place, the nation conducting a power policy has an interest in diverting its trade to poor countries in which the marginal utility of income is high. Thus, if nation A, embarking on a power policy, has had a certain amount of trade with group B of other rich industrial nations, it might of course try to enlarge its influence in these countries by granting them better terms of trade. But this would interfere with its own production and, in addition, these countries might not value very highly the additional supplies coming from A. If, on the other hand, the nation diverts its trade to group C of poor and agricultural countries from which it can receive the same supplies, the gain from trade obtained by group C will exceed what group B's gain had been, and consequently A's influence in group C will be much greater than it was in group B. Although the real costs of the supplies may be higher in group C than in group B, A will then have little difficulty in manipulating the terms of trade in such a way that she gives no more of her home produce in exchange for her imports than formerly.

Renewed attention has been given recently to the analysis of ex-

---

[18] We assume here, as stated in the beginning of this section (p. 17), that only the country conducting a power policy is at liberty to choose its trading partners, whereas the latter have no option but to trade with that country. This assumption will be dropped below. Here we also disregard the fact that the power-seeking nation may prefer to obtain a small influence in a neighboring state rather than a large one in a distant country. In a sense, our analysis considers every country as an equally interesting object of a power policy. Total influence is for us the sum of the influences secured in the individual countries, whereas actually every influence should be weighted according to strategic or other considerations. But this means only that the role played by the economic determinants of power must eventually be combined with and be qualified by the other determinants. The reader must judge whether the results reached by our analysis warrant the admittedly artificial isolation of the economic factor.

ploitation, both with respect to the factor of production in the domestic economy and to that of one country by another in international economic relations. For the latter subject it has been shown what conditions and what policies are required for a country to turn the terms of trade in its favor. At the outset this type of inquiry seems to be the exact opposite of our analysis of the influence effect, which depends on the gain from trade of the trading *partners*. The possibility of a conflict between the policy of maximization of national income, on the one hand, and the policy of securing the greatest position of influence with the trading partners, on the other, certainly deserves to be pointed out. But our subsequent analysis has shown that these two types of policies are not necessarily alternatives. The successful pursuit of the one policy may even condition the emergence of the other. The ability to manipulate the terms of trade in one's favor depends, indeed, on the gain from trade derived by the trading partners, and the policies we have described are directed precisely to increase this gain. The monopolistic exploitation of a trading partner can then be considered as one of the uses to which the power secured through the influence effect may be put. We are here concerned only with the methods and conditions leading to this power, not with its possible uses which may be the reaping of advantages of any kind—military and political, as well as economic.

ADJUSTMENT DIFFICULTIES AND VESTED INTERESTS

The threat of an interruption of trade—the ever-present characteristic of commerce between sovereign states—has two main effects upon the economy of the country the trade of which is interrupted: It impoverishes this country and also imposes a process of adjustment, since, when imports are no longer forthcoming, the goods formerly exported will no longer be consumed in the home market. Marshall's definition of the gain from trade: the excess of utility of the imports over the utility of the goods produced by the resources otherwise devoted to exports if there were no imports—compares the utilities of two nonsimultaneous sets of goods and thus obviously includes a time element. The immediate loss from the stoppage of trade is much greater than the ultimate loss after resources have been fully reallocated. The classical theory of international trade was aware of this distinction;[19] but it concentrated upon the ultimate loss and considered the time elapsing from interruption of trade to reallocation of resources within the country as a short-run period. Modern theory insists that this is not necessarily true; and even if it were true, our analysis would have to take into account the fact that harassed statesmen generally have a short-run view. Given a certain ultimate loss, the influence which one country exercises upon another through foreign trade is therefore likely to be larger the greater the immediate loss which it can inflict by a stoppage of trade.

For a country cut off from foreign trade the most urgent problem is to produce at home or to find substitutes for goods which were formerly imported and to find new employment for the factors of production formerly employed in export industries. The first problem is definitely connected with the ultimate loss from the interruption of trade, whereas the second is a short-run problem. Nevertheless, the "danger of losing a market" if political conditions deteriorate makes for as much concern as the danger of losing supplies. According to classical theory the active side of the gain from trade derives only from the imports, and the exports are set as a passive item against them. Modern theory, on the other hand, has presented an analysis which, within the framework of a national policy aiming at full employment, considers exports as an incentive to employment and national income, and imports as "leakages" which to a certain degree prevent the working of this incentive.[20] The classical and the modern approaches are of course based on quite different assumptions, and each is valuable in its own field for the explanation of some relevant economic facts. The modern approach, with its emphasis on immobility, overhead costs, and incomplete use of resources, leads to an understanding of why the common belief that the real benefit arising from trade lies in exports rather than imports is more than a mere "popular fallacy."

Obviously, the difficulties arising out of a cessation of exports will be greater the greater the exports (and consequently the imports); and the short-run problem is thus intimately connected with the extent of the long-run gain from trade. But with a given quantity

---

[19] Ricardo, in his *Principles of Political Economy*, states it thus at the beginning of the chapter on "Sudden Changes in the Channels of Trade."

[20] For a discussion of the "Foreign Trade Multiplier," see Gottfried Haberler, *Prosperity and Depression*, 3d ed. (Geneva, 1942), pp. 461–473, and literature quoted in that work.

of exports the problem created by an interruption of trade will be the more difficult, (1) the smaller the mobility of resources within the country, (2) the more the economic activities leading to exports have been concentrated in certain lines of production or in certain regions.

The mobility of resources includes the possibility of diverting capital goods to new purposes (i.e., their more or less "specific" character), the geographical mobility of the factors of production, and, above all, the ability of labor to turn to new tasks. The inherent advantage with respect to all these aspects of the mobility of resources lies overwhelmingly with the great manufacturing and trading countries as opposed to countries in which agriculture or mining predominates. Here again the prevention of industrialization would be the aim of a power trying to make the adjustment problem appear insoluble to the countries with which it trades.[21]

The second factor having a definite bearing upon the relative ease of adjustment after an interruption of trade is the extent to which production for export is concentrated in certain products or in certain regions. If most of the exports are made up of one particular product, there is very little probability that any great part of it can be consumed at home if the foreign outlet fails; if the exports all come from certain specialized regions within the country, there will be "distressed areas" and a need for large-scale relief and resettlement. It is highly unlikely that the pattern of the economic activities devoted to exports will follow closely the distribution of general economic activity among geographical regions and lines of production. But the discrepancy of the two patterns may be more or less pronounced, and, accordingly, the contribution of exports to dependence upon foreign trade will be large or small.

This subject is directly linked with the vested interests created by trade: a greater concern with the maintenance and expansion of trade in certain quarters than in the country as a whole. The actual going volume of trade, indeed, produces its own vested interests,

---

[21] We are considering the mobility of resources only so far as it influences the distribution of power created by foreign trade. Of course the mobility of resources has an extremely important *direct* bearing upon political and economic power. This aspect has been pointed out very clearly by Mr. Hawtrey, *op. cit.*, pp. 83–92. For a good discussion of the various factors influencing the mobility of resources within an industrialized country with special reference to the trade cycle, see C. M. Wright, *Economic Adaptation to a Changing World Market*, Chapter V (Copenhagen, 1939).

just as does the limitation of trade through protection; and the history of commercial policy offers convincing evidence that the protectionists would have been still more successful than they have been if they had had to contend only with the opposition of the "consumers at large."

If conditions are such that the possible loss from a stoppage of trade would fall with special weight upon certain groups within the country, these groups are likely to form a sort of "commercial fifth column." Aside from the purely commercial groups, such as import and export companies, the influence of which is generally meager, the vested interests will consist of the producers for export and of the industries using imported raw materials. If exports are concentrated in some region or some industry, not only will the difficulty of adjustment in the case of loss of these exports weigh upon the decisions of the government, but these regions or industries will exert a powerful influence in favor of a "friendly" attitude toward the state to the imports of which they owe their existence. Creation of potential adjustment difficulties and of vested interests is thus the twofold result of a commercial policy which aims at an intensive specialization of the trading partner's economy and which tries to prevent the diversification of the partner's exports with respect to regions and to products. In the social pattern of each country there exist certain powerful groups the support of which is particularly valuable to a *foreign* country in its power policy; the foreign country will therefore try to establish commercial relations especially with these groups, in order that their voices will be raised in its favor.

THE INFLUENCE EFFECT OF FOREIGN TRADE (SECTION 2)

We must now drop a simplifying assumption under which we have worked hitherto and allow for the possibility of alternative markets or sources of supply. A country menaced with an interruption of trade with a given country has the alternative of diverting its trade to a third country; by so doing it evades more or less completely the damaging consequences of the stoppage of its trade with one particular country. The stoppage or the threat of it would thus lose all its force. In order to prevent this, the country wishing to conserve the influence derived from foreign trade in the real world of many nations must therefore take some precautions. The prin-

ciples which we have formulated for power policy through the
instrumentality of foreign trade retain their full validity. They were
aimed at rendering it difficult for the other countries to *dispense*
with foreign trade; but if we wish these principles to be effective in
the real world, they must be supplemented by measures which make
it difficult for other countries to *shift* the trade conducted with them
by the nation trying to increase its power by foreign trade.

Any switching of trade would, of course, be rendered impossible
by a monopoly of trade imposed by one nation upon another. In
the old colonial system a colony was not permitted to turn to other
buyers or sellers, even though the mother country had no obligation
at all to provide the colony with goods or to buy from it. Under
modern conditions subtler methods must be devised in order to
arrive at similar results. A country may still hope to create conditions in which the diversion of trade to a third country will be much
more difficult for its partner than for itself.[22]

In a very general way the difficulty of substituting country A as a
market or supply source for country B may be said to depend not
only on the absolute amount of A's trade with B, but also on the
importance of this trade relatively to B's total trade. If, for instance,
a country loses 5 per cent of its export trade, it should be able to
find additional outlets in the markets which account normally for
95 per cent of its exports and where a sales organization for its products is likely to exist already. Similarly, if the country loses a relatively small fraction of its import trade, it is probable not only that
its economic activity is not based to an undue degree upon these
supplies, but also that other countries will be able and eager to
make up for them. The greater the percentage of exports and imports involved in a dominant market, the more difficult it will be
to provide substitute markets and sources of supply.

If a nation with an absolutely large volume of trade imports from,
or exports to, a small trading nation, the trade they conduct together will inevitably result in a much higher percentage for the
small than for the large trading nation. German-Bulgarian trade in
1938, for example, represented 52 and 59 per cent of Bulgarian
imports and exports, respectively, but only 1.5 and 1.1 per cent of

---

[22] How important this problem is even in simple commercial bargaining is repeatedly
brought out by N. F. Hall, "Trade Diversion—An Australian Interlude," *Economica,*
Vol. V, new series (February, 1938).

the German imports and exports. These figures indicate that although the same absolute amount is involved, it will be much more difficult for Bulgaria to shift her trade with Germany to other countries than it will be for Germany to replace Bulgaria as a selling market and a source of supplies.[23] In the real world of many sovereign states it will therefore be an elementary principle of the power policy of a state to *direct its trade away from the large to the smaller trading states.* This principle must then be added to the one established above, viz., that trade should be directed toward the poorer countries. The two are by no means contradictory, as there are many states which are both poor and small.

Similarly, it will be an elementary defensive principle of the smaller trading countries not to have too large a share of their trade with any single great trading country, so that the integration of their economies with those of the great countries (for which no reciprocal integration is forthcoming) may be kept at a minimum compatible with their economic well-being. The idea that dependence can be diminished by distributing the trade among many countries has been clearly enunciated by Macaulay. These two principles, the one offensive for the large countries, the other defensive for the small countries, gave rise to the first two inquiries of our statistical section.

A more specific policy by which a country could try to prevent its trading partners from diverting their trade to other countries would consist in the creation of monopolistic or monopsonistic conditions with regard to certain products.[24]

With respect to exports, country A may try to change the structure of country B's economy so as to make it highly and artificially complementary to A's own economy. First, A may encourage the production of products having but little demand in other countries. This amounts to the creation of what might be called "exclusive complementarity" between the economy of country B and country A.

Furthermore, country B may have a comparative advantage in the production of a certain commodity with respect to country A, but not with respect to countries C, D, E, etc. If by some preferential

---

[23] Not only is it more difficult for Bulgaria than for Germany to shift trade, but it is also harder for Bulgaria to *dispense* entirely with the trade conducted with Germany, because this trade is much more "essential" to her. This is, however, not a consequence of her comparative smallness, but of factors pointed out in section 1 of this chapter.

[24] Cf. H. K. Heuser, *The Control of International Trade* (London, 1939), pp. 250–251.

treatment, A induced B to produce this commodity for export, A becomes B's only market, and the dependence of B upon A thus created may be well worth to A the economic cost involved in not buying in the cheapest market. In general, any attempt to drive the prices of exports from trading partners above world prices, whether by the direct encouragement of production contrary to the comparative cost principle or by general monetary manipulations, will fit in with the policy of increasing their dependence.

The paying of a higher price is only the most obvious way of rendering more arduous the diversion of a trading partner's exports to third markets. The offer of some special advantage relating to the conditions of the contract other than the price works toward the same effect. Firms often reward loyalty on the part of their customers by rebates and other devices.[25] The economies of regularity and the considerations of risk which explain this practice play an even greater role in foreign trade; with prices uniform, exports will therefore be directed preferably to those countries which are able and willing to guarantee stable prices for a prolonged period.

With respect to imports, the substitution of the imported products from any country will be more difficult in the absence of a natural monopoly the more highly differentiated are the products. Such products tend to create fixed consumption habits and production techniques, and difficulties arise when these products have to be replaced by similar but not identical products from other countries. Hence, it is generally easier for an industrial country to change the source of its supply of foodstuffs and raw materials than it is for a country producing foodstuffs or raw materials to change its traditional supplier of industrial goods.[26]

Under conditions of incomplete use of resources, however, it will generally be much easier to switch imports than exports, all countries being ready to sell and none ready to buy. This fact has indeed tended to dominate the whole discussion of the determinants of bargaining power between two trading countries. It was held that superior bargaining power is *always* on the side of the country having a passive trade balance with its trading partner. In other words,

[25] Cf. W. A. Lewis, "Notes on the Economics of Loyalty," *Economica*, Vol. IX, new series (November, 1942), pp. 333–348.

[26] Cf. R. F. Harrod's distinction of A, B, and C goods in his *International Economics*, new ed. (London, 1939), pp. 60 ff.

the difficulty of shifting imports was entirely discounted, whereas in assessing the difficulty of shifting exports no account was taken of the various factors enumerated above. It was thought that the country having the greater absolute volume of exports would automatically experience the greater difficulties of diversion and thereby find itself in an inferior bargaining position.[27] This is, of course, far too great a simplification; but the fact remains that an intelligent power policy must take account of the greater difficulty which is generally experienced in diverting exports.

Let us suppose then that country A buys a percentage of B's exports sufficiently large to render a substitution of these exports well-nigh impossible for B. Is there any means of extending this impossibility to the switching of B's imports as well? We see immediately that the policy of bilateralism is perfectly fitted to take care of this problem. Indeed, under conditions of bilateralism, a real impossibility of switching exports induces a *technical* impossibility of switching imports. In this way the device of bilateralism is seen to be an important link in the policies by which the aim of maximum power through foreign trade may be attained.

In all our analysis we have spoken exclusively of direct import and export trade. *Transit trade* plays a special and somewhat contradictory role when we try to answer the question: Should a country, from the point of view of power policy, aim at a large transit trade? On the one hand it would seem that transit trade can always be replaced by direct trade and that therefore the country handling the transit trade is in a rather weak position. But if the replacement of the transit trade is impracticable for geographical, technical, or contractural reasons, transit trade is immediately seen to be an ideal means of increasing power by trade. Indeed, the economy of the country handling this trade is only superficially affected by the trade; whereas it acquires the influence normally deriving from exports and imports both in the country of origin and the country of final destination of the transit commodities. In other words, pro-

---

[27] Relatively early the German economist Dietzel attacked this view: "In respect to the question of the strength of the (bargaining) position, it does not matter so much which one of the two nations waging a tariff war buys more from the other; it matters more which of the two nations can better do without the market of the other, and is able in the case of loss of this market, to sell nearly as much elsewhere."—Karl Dietzel, *Der deutsch-amerikanische Handelsvertrag und das Phantom der amerikanischen Industriekonkurrenz* (Berlin, 1905), p. 20.

vided only that its services are indispensable, the country handling the transit trade acquires from that trade a twofold influence and at the same time evades almost entirely any dependence of its own economy.

AN ILLUSTRATION: GERMAN TRADING METHODS UNDER NATIONAL SOCIALISM

The conditions or policies which have been described as being conducive to increased national power by means of foreign trade can be summarized by the following synoptical table:

Principles of a Power Policy Using Foreign Trade as Its Instrument

I. Policies relying on the *supply effect* of foreign trade and trying to insure its working even in times of war.

    A. Concentrate imports on goods needed for the war machine.

    B. Accumulate large stocks of strategic materials.

    C. Redirect trade to neighboring politically friendly or subject nations.

    D. Secure control of the oceanic trade routes.

II. Policies relying on the *influence effect* of foreign trade.

    A. Policies designed to make it more difficult for the trading partner to *dispense entirely* with the trade.

        1. Increase the trading partners' gain from trade (without impairing the supply effect).

            a. Develop exports in articles enjoying a monopolistic position in other countries and direct trade to such countries.

            b. Direct trade toward poorer countries.

        2. Increase the trading partners' adjustment difficulties in case of stoppage of trade.

            a. Trade with countries with little mobility of resources.

            b. Induce a wide discrepancy between the pattern of production for exports and the pattern of production for home consumption.

        3. Create vested interests and tie the interests of existing powerful groups to the trade.

    B. Policies designed to make it difficult for the trading partners to *shift* trade to each other or to third countries.

        1. In general: Direct trade toward the small trading countries.

2. With respect to the exports of the trading partners:
   a. Import products for which there is little demand in other countries.
   b. Drive prices of the export products of the trading partners above world prices:
      i. By fostering high-cost production.
      ii. By monetary manipulations.
   c. Grant to the trading partners' exports advantages not relating to the price of their products.
3. With respect to the imports of the trading partners:
   a. Export highly differentiated goods creating consumption and production habits.
   b. Develop trade on a bilateral basis.
4. Develop transit trade.

Practically all the outstanding features of German foreign economic policy since 1933 can be subsumed under this scheme. This does not mean, as will be explained below, that Germany has consciously worked out such a master plan. Keeping this in mind from the outset, we shall show very briefly the correspondence in each point between German policies and the general principles of a power policy through foreign trade which we have established. We shall list the German policies in the order indicated by the synoptical table and refer back to it each time by its own symbols. In our account of German policies, we rely on numerous studies of German trading methods to which the reader may turn for full information.[28]

[28] Antonin Basch, *The New Economic Warfare*, Chapter I (New York, 1941); H. M. Bratter, "Foreign Exchange Control in Latin America," *Foreign Policy Reports* (February 15, 1939); J. B. Condliffe, *The Reconstruction of World Trade* (New York, 1940), pp. 256–262, 291–294, 323–324; "Germany's Trade Offensive," *The Economist* (London, November 5, 1938); Paul Einzig, *Bloodless Invasion* (London, 1938); Howard S. Ellis, *Exchange Control in Central Europe* (Cambridge, Mass., 1941); A. G. B. Fisher, "The German Trade Drive in South-Eastern Europe," *International Affairs*, Vol. XVIII (March-April, 1939); Margaret S. Gordon, *Barriers to World Trade*, Part IV (New York, 1941); H. C. Hillmann, "Analysis of Germany's Foreign Trade and the War," *Economica*, new series, Vol. VII (February, 1940); *Europe's Trade* (League of Nations, Geneva, 1941); Fritz Meyer, "Devisenbewirtschaftung als neue Währungsform," *Weltwirtschaftliches Archiv*, Vol. XLIX (May, 1939); von Mickwitz, "The Economic Structure of Capital Exports to South-Eastern Europe," Mimeographed for the International Studies Conference (Bergen, 1939); Douglas Miller, *"You Can't Do Business With Hitler* (New York, 1941); Mark Mitnitzky, "Germany's Trade Monopoly in Eastern Europe," *Social Research*, Vol. VI (February, 1939); *South-Eastern Europe* (Royal Institute of International Affairs, London, 1939); *South-Eastern Europe* (Royal Institute of International Affairs, London, December, 1940), (this is a separate and distinct work from the previous same-named publication); Hans Staudinger, "The Future of Totalitarian Barter Trade," *Social Research*, Vol. VII (November, 1940).

Little need be said concerning the policies relating to the supply effect of foreign trade. Germany considered her exports a means of obtaining in exchange certain imports deemed essential for her purposes (I A.); she accumulated large stocks of strategic materials (I B.); and she directed her trade toward countries from which she hoped not to be cut off in the case of war (I C.). The two latter policies, coupled with the autarkic program, were considered as a substitute for the control of the oceanic trade routes (I D.) which Germany could not hope to achieve.

Let us now turn to the influence effect. Germany's attempt to concentrate on exports of finished products, on the one hand, and on exports to agricultural countries, on the other, had obviously the result of giving her exports a quasi-monopolistic position so far as the productive system of her trading partners was concerned (II A.1.a.). In addition, to maintain this position, it was one of the great principles of German foreign economic policy to prevent the industrialization of her agricultural trading partners. Particular insistence on this point has been noted in all the commercial negotiations of Germany with her southeastern neighbors and even, to some degree and some success, with Italy.

The policy of trading with agricultural countries and, furthermore, of preventing the establishment of industries in these countries is indeed prompted, not only by the consideration just mentioned, but also by the fact that agricultural countries have generally but little mobility of resources (II A.2.a.), and that manufactured products, being highly differentiated, are often difficult to replace immediately by similar products from other countries (II B.3.a.). Here we have an example of the above-mentioned cumulative effect of power. Germany could never have hampered or prevented the industrialization of the Danubian countries if she had not had an initial political and economic ascendancy over them, and the prevention of industrialization in turn served to enhance or to maintain Germany's initial power position.

The modification of the structure of German trade can also be interpreted as a shift of trade from the relatively rich to the relatively poor countries (II A.1.b.). In order to give a statistical illustration, we have computed the shares in German trade for the eleven countries which, according to the thesis expounded by Colin Clark, are "richer" than Germany in the sense that real income per head of the employed population is higher.[29]

Looking at the percentages of the single countries, one notices that, with the exception of Eire, Denmark, and Sweden, an all-round decrease from 1929 to 1938 is evident. For Denmark and Sweden the incentive of regionalism may have outweighed other considerations. The trade with Eire is relatively insignificant.

The policy of trading with countries having but little mobility of resources (II A.2.a.) has already been commented upon. Germany has also induced the southeastern countries to use still more resources in the production of certain crops (oil seeds, fiber plants)

SHARES HELD BY ELEVEN COUNTRIES "RICHER" THAN GERMANY
IN TOTAL GERMAN IMPORT AND EXPORT TRADE*

Year	Imports per cent	Exports per cent
1929	41.9	49.0
1932	39.1	48.9
1937	29.9	38.6
1938	31.3	37.1

* In 1938 Austria is excluded from the foreign trade statistics. In order to make the figures for the other years comparable to those of 1938, Austria has been excluded throughout, i.e., the figures are percentages of the total German trade minus Austrian trade. The figures have been computed from German sources (*Statistisches Jahrbuch für das Deutsche Reich* and *Wirtschaft und Statistik*).

and mineral resources which would practically be exported in their entirety (II A.2.b.). By offering a stable market for the agricultural surplus production of these countries, she tied landowners and peasants, the most powerful social groups in these countries, to her own interests (II A.3.).

Coming to the policies rendering a diversion of trade more difficult for the trading partners, we shall show in Chapter V how Germany concentrated her trade on the relatively small trading countries (II B.1.). The fostering of special products such as oil seeds and fiber plants is also an example of the creation of exports for which there would be little demand in other countries (II B.2.a.). Germany's encouragement of cultivation of cotton in Brazil, Tur-

[29] Colin Clark, *The Conditions of Economic Progress* (London, 1940), p. 41. The eleven countries are, in the order indicated by the author: United States, Canada, New Zealand, Great Britain, Switzerland, Australia, Holland, Eire, France, Denmark, Sweden. The margin of error of such calculations is admittedly very wide, but, over a short range of years, a computation such as we give on this page may serve our purposes.

key, and Greece, and her exploitation of low-grade mineral resources in Rumania and Yugoslavia can be shown to be contrary to the comparative cost principle (II B.2.b.i.). In general, Germany supported the agricultural economies of southeastern Europe without insisting upon the adjustments necessary to render them competitive on a world level. This had the effect of adding to basic cost disequilibria a monetary disequilibrium which drove the price system of these countries upward by the device of overvaluation of the reichsmark (II B.2.b.ii.). In this connection it must also be recalled that Germany has not only paid prices higher than those which could be had in the world market, but that trade with Germany offered to the southeastern countries another substantial advantage over trade with other countries: Germany had promised to these countries conditions of stability in both price and volume of their exports (II B.2.c.).[30]

With respect to imports which create consumption and production habits (II B.3.a.), we have already mentioned the general advantage of industrial countries in comparison with agricultural countries. The export of armaments to the Balkan countries, extensively practiced by Germany, is an item very much to the point, since a retraining of personnel is a necessary accompaniment of any improved style or variety of arms. In addition, once the main weapons had been accepted from Germany, the importing countries had to rely on her for ammunition and spare and repair parts. Bilateralism (II B.3.b.) has not only been the most evident new principle introduced by Germany into trade relations, but it has also had exactly the same function which we have attributed to it in our exposition: forcing the countries selling a substantial share of their exports to Germany to grant Germany a similarly dominating position in their imports. Finally, Germany has made the most sustained efforts to increase the amount of transit trade which she traditionally handled as a result of her geographical position (II B.4.). She tried to sell to the world the Balkan products, and to the Balkans she attempted to sell such "colonial" products as coffee, cocoa, etc.

---

[30] There is nothing paradoxical about the fact that the power of the state to interrupt trade may be made into a more effective weapon by granting to its trading partners certain advantages, e.g., of security—for a time. The security, indeed, is revokable; and the power of the state granting security in trade relations is precisely born of the desire of its trading partners to prevent the loss of this security. Here again *fortuna est servitus*.

The correspondence between German policies and the principles of a power policy carried on through foreign trade, which we have deduced from simple premises, will now have become clear. Just as these principles were originally derived by us from the single postulate of maximum power, German policies can be understood as a coherent whole by reference to this postulate.

Only future research into the proceedings of the inner councils of Nazi leaders will show how far their plans for economic conquest were actually laid down in advance. It seems probable, however, that the amazing coherence of German policies was due only in part to detailed planning springing from economic analysis and that an important role was left to experimentation in the elaboration of actual policies. But if we assume only that in every decision of commercial policy the political power standpoint was given due consideration, the coherence of German policies need not surprise us, for, in every case, this power, so far as it is based on foreign trade at all, goes back in the last analysis either to the strength which foreign trade lends to the German war machine (supply effect) or to Germany's power to menace her trading partners with a stoppage of trade (influence effect). It is therefore only natural that by examining in a general way the processes through which these two sources of power through foreign trade could be best developed, we should at the same time have described the actual policies of a state which had made power the primary object of its actions in every field.

It will have been noted that a single policy such as the prevention of industrialization realized simultaneously several distinct features of the power policy outlined in different parts of the present analysis. Similarly, we have seen how an apparent conflict between the supply effect and the influence effect of foreign trade could find a solution. Furthermore, a shift of trade toward the poorer countries will often be found to implement the other principle of power policy which impels a country to divert its trade toward the smaller trading countries. All these instances tend to show that there is a real danger of attributing too much cleverness to German policy by supposing a motive behind certain effects of policy which, though welcome, may not have been actually aimed at.

Economists have often dwelt upon situations in which a policy is self-defeating, i.e., leads to certain unforeseen repercussions which foil the aim at which the policy was originally directed. It is, however, equally possible that a policy has unforeseen effects which reinforce rather than destroy the result which the policy had tried to bring about. It may well be—here again only future documents will give us an even approximate knowledge—that in German trading methods we are confronted by precisely such a situation. This would detract somewhat from our opinion of the thoroughness and the astuteness of the Nazis, but it would also raise in our minds a question of grave importance: Are the conditions in the actual world such as to make the pursuit of power a relatively easy task?

Undoubtedly, conflicts between the policies implementing the different principles of a power policy with foreign trade as an instrument are conceivable and do occur; but they seem to be less important than the situations in which it is possible to realize concurrently several power objectives by a single policy.

Finally, it must be remembered that the conditions which we have described as leading to power relationships are not necessarily brought about by any conscious policy at all. Indeed, the initial impetus to German policies in the 'thirties was given even before Hitler's advent to power, not by political motives, but by the economic fact that Germany, a debtor country with a weak currency, found herself attracted to the central and southeastern European countries which were in a similar position. The important point is that power elements and disequilibria are potentially inherent in such "harmless" trade relations as have always taken place, e.g., between big and small, rich and poor, agricultural and industrial countries—relations which could be fully in accord with the principles taught by the theory of international trade. Political power may only be latent in such commercial relations. But so long as war remains a possibility and so long as the sovereign nation can interrupt trade with any country at its own will, the contest for more national power permeates trade relations, and foreign trade provides an opportunity for power which it will be tempting to seize.

NOTES ON THE THEORY OF INTERNATIONAL TRADE

The following remarks serve to elaborate for the technical reader certain questions in the theory of international trade connected with the analysis given in the preceding pages.

EQUILIBRIUM IN INTERNATIONAL TRADE UNDER VARYING
ASSUMPTIONS IN THE INSTITUTIONAL FRAMEWORK[31]

For our purpose it is useful to distinguish between three types of
trade organization *within* a given country:

   a) Competitive conditions and absence of any state intervention;
   b) Competitive conditions and possibility of unilateral state intervention, e.g., imposition of tariffs;
   c) State monopoly of foreign trade.

If we contemplate trade between two states, trade may be carried
on under any one of six possible combinations. But only four of
these, which might be called aa, bb, cc, and ab, need be analyzed.
If we assume that the trade is in two commodities, the apparatus of
the Marshallian foreign trade curves, together with the theory of
bilateral monopoly developed by Edgeworth, Pigou, and Bowley,[32]
permit us to illustrate these cases by a simple diagrammatical device.

In figure 1 the abscissa measures the amounts of a commodity
produced by country X, and the ordinate the amounts of another
commodity produced by country Y. OQ_1 is the indifference curve
of X, showing the bargains which would leave X as badly off as if
it did not trade at all. Let us call this curve, with Professor Viner,[33]
the *no-gain-from-trade curve*. To this curve, correspond other indifference curves which will cut the Y ordinate (the dotted curves
in our figure). A similar indifference map exists for Y, and OQ_2 is
Y's no-gain-from-trade curve. The locus of the points at which any
two indifference curves of these two systems are tangential to each
other is the curve Q_1Q_2, which is called the contract curve in the
theory of bilateral monopoly. The curve OP_1P is a Marshallian supply-demand curve, i.e., the locus of the points at which straight lines
drawn in any direction from the origin and indicating a certain position of the terms of trade touch the indifference curves of Y. The

---

[31] A very interesting article by Tibor de Scitovsky, "A Reconsideration of the Theory
of Tariffs," *Review of Economic Studies*, Vol. IX (Summer, 1942), has come to my notice
after the above notes had been written. De Scitovsky's main contribution is an elucida-
tion of the precise meaning of community-indifference curves; but he also gives (*ibid.*,
pp. 102–105) a comparison of trade under barter agreements and of trade when tariffs
are the main weapon of commercial policy, which has much in common with the
analysis presented here.
[32] Cf. bibliography given by Gerhard Tintner, "Note on the Problem of Bilateral
Monopoly," *Journal of Political Economy*, Vol. XLVII (April, 1939), p. 263.
[33] Viner, *op. cit.*, p. 576.

curve OP$_2$P is the corresponding locus for X. The supply-demand
curve of Y (OP$_1$P) touches an indifference curve of X at the point
P$_1$, and similarly the supply-demand curve of X (OP$_2$P) touches an
indifference curve of Y at P$_2$. We can now proceed to the analysis
of the various cases.

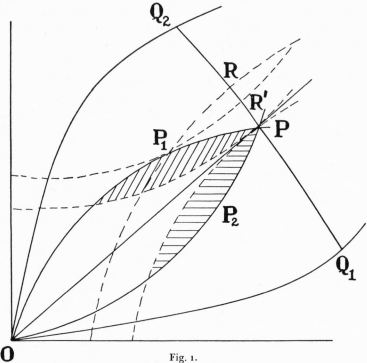

Fig. 1.

Case aa (classical case of perfect competition): Every party considers the terms of trade as a datum and moves along its supply-
demand curve until the quantity offered is equal to the quantity
demanded. Determinate equilibrium is established at P. It can be
proved that P lies on the contract curve.

Case cc (classical case of bilateral monopoly): The terms of trade
lose their regulatory function and two monopolists drive a bargain
which will lie somewhere on the contract curve. This curve is, indeed, the locus for all bargains which, with a given satisfaction from
trade of the one partner, maximize the satisfaction of the other.
Which particular point will be arrived at by the two countries trading together depends on "bargaining power."

Case ab (foreign trade between two countries, each of which has a competitive trading system, but only one, say X, enjoying tariff autonomy, which is an attribute of sovereignty): In this case the terms of trade lose their regulatory function for country X, but not for Y. Like any monopolist, country X can aim at evaluating the demand curve of its trading partner and at finding out the point most advantageous from its own standpoint.[34] This point is P_1, at which, as we said before, an indifference curve of X touches the supply-demand curve of Y. By imposing a duty upon its goods, X will be able to shift its demand curve so that it cuts Y's demand curve at precisely this point. It is not possible here to compare the total utility obtained at P and that obtained at P_1 by the two trading countries taken together. All one can say is that at P_1, X is better off and Y worse off than at P. But by drawing the indifference curves going through P_1 until they cut the contract curve at R and at R', we see that there is a stretch, RR', on the contract curve, each point of which offers to both parties more satisfaction than either can obtain at P_1.

Case bb:[35] If both countries have full economic sovereignty whilst retaining their competitive trading system, they may both try to influence the terms of trade by the imposition of tariffs. In other words, so far as the absence of the parametric function of price for the country as a whole is concerned, the position is very similar to case cc, in which the theory of bilateral monopoly became applicable. Obviously, with any given system of tariff rates, equilibrium is again determinate. But although tariff rates have the same economic effect as transport costs, the usual procedure of simply including tariffs among the data of international economic equilibrium seems illegitimate, the reasons for which we will presently point out.

The history of commercial negotiations gives abundant proof that tariffs are the manifestation of bargaining power under conditions of private trading. If tariffs are considered as data, bargaining power should in all cases be treated in the same way, and equilib-

---

[34] This has been recently recalled by Nicholas Kaldor, "A Note on Tariffs and the Terms of Trade," *Economica*, Vol. VII, new series (November, 1940), pp. 379–380.

[35] Cf., in connection with the following section, the article of A. C. Pigou, "Equilibrium under Bilateral Monopoly," *Economic Journal*, Vol. XVIII (1908), pp. 205 ff. Although our approach has much in common with Pigou's analysis, Pigou was not interested in the applications of the theory of bilateral monopoly to international trade, but rather to wage theory.

rium under conditions of bilateral monopoly would be perfectly determinate. If, on the other hand, tariffs are not treated as data, equilibrium in our case is just as indeterminate as it was in case cc. In other words, even with entirely competitive markets, the institution of national economic sovereignty implants elements of monopoly and indeterminateness in the trading system.

This indeterminateness is, however, different in kind from that which we have analyzed under cc. Every country can influence the terms of trade by the imposition of tariffs. But once this has been done, the market is left to adjust itself to the new conditions. The price and the terms of trade remain objective data for the traders, and therefore the equilibrium positions all lie on the possible intersections of the supply and demand curves as modified by government intervention. Since an imposition of a duty on exports or a subsidy on imports may be considered unlikely, the Marshallian curves will shift nearer to each other. We obtain thus a surface of indeterminateness, OP_2PP_1, bounded by the two original curves of case aa. Any point lying on the surface, including the point of origin, may be the outcome of successive impositions of tariffs. The shaded area indicates the possible position at which one of the two trading partners will be better off than at the free trade position P. At all other points of the surface both countries would be worse off than they were before they started to impose tariffs and to retaliate. What we pointed out for point P_1 in connection with case ab holds here generally also. For every point of the surface OP_2PP_1 (with the exception of P) there exists a segment on the contract curve every point of which yields to both countries a higher amount of satisfaction. The imposition of tariffs is therefore seen to be a rather inefficient weapon for a country desiring to obtain an increase in satisfaction from a movement of the terms of trade in its favor. It seems a significant confirmation of the foregoing analysis that countries which have had a foreign economic policy which considers exports as a means to obtain imports (and not imports as a necessary evil to secure export markets) have generally reverted from a tariff policy to a policy of direct bargaining.

There exists, then, a difference between a policy relying on autonomous tariffs and a policy of direct state trading. But this difference is far from being as fundamental as has often been believed. Autonomous tariff policy, we have shown, introduces into the international market elements of indeterminateness which differ from such elements under bilateral monopoly mainly in the fact that they lead to a range of possibilities which, from the standpoint of the satisfaction of both countries, is much inferior to the range offered by bargaining of two countries each with a foreign trade monopoly. In addition, our analysis shows that, by supposing international trade to result in determinate equilibrium, the theory of international trade assumes, not only perfect competition, but also the absence of economic sovereignty.

A NOTE ON BARGAINING POWER

In the theory of bilateral monopoly the term bargaining power has a definite technical meaning. It denotes the forces which, with given indifference systems of the two monopolists, make for equilibrium at one rather than another point on the contract curve. The components of bargaining power in this sense are somewhat vague; they are generally believed to be bargaining skill, information on the indifference system of the partner, deception of the partner about one's own indifference system, and simple force, which, however, is limited by the shape of the partner's no-gain-from-trade curve. Indeed, it is not possible for either of the monopolists to exploit the other in the sense that by exchange the one is made to be less well off than he was before the exchange took place. It is not even possible to draw from the location of the equilibrium point on the contract curve any conclusion for a comparison of the advantages derived by the two monopolists from the exchange. If, for instance, the exchange takes place at the center of the contract curve, we could say that the advantages derived by both monopolists are equal only if we assume: (1) that the indifference systems of the two monopolists are identical, and (2) that the two no-gain-from-trade curves express equal levels of satisfaction for both monopolists.

It would therefore be incorrect to say that superior bargaining power enables one monopolist to gain more satisfaction than his partner; all we may affirm is that it enables him to increase his gain at the expense of that of his partner.

The term bargaining power is, however, used in contexts implying a different meaning. Thus, if we say that the bargaining power of the entrepreneur is superior to that of the nonunionized worker—considered as an individual factor of production with some elasticity of substitution—we think not only of the differences in bargaining skill, cunning, information, etc., but mainly of the fact that the worker "needs" the entrepreneur more than the entrepreneur "needs" him. This, in turn, means that we are here implicitly comparing two utility gains or, at least, the levels of satisfaction of the two opponents if there is no contract. Similarly, if we say that adherence to a trade union enhances the bargaining power of the worker, we imply not only that the trade union has more information, skill in negotiation, etc., than the individual worker could possibly have, but also that the wage at which it would be a matter of indifference to the worker to be idle or to work is higher after than before his adherence to the union. We have here essentially a dynamic problem, since the indifference system of the worker is supposed to have shifted so as to form a *new contract curve* with the indifference system of the entrepreneur. Even if the bargaining skill of the two parties has remained the same, the wage will be higher under the new conditions because the range of possibilities offered by the new contract curve to the worker is better than the old one.[36]

In other words, there are two methods to better one's position: either by working toward a better point on a given contract curve, or by bringing about a new and more favorably situated contract curve. This latter aim may be realized, as in the familiar case of unionization, by shifting one's own indifference system, i.e., by enabling the worker, backed by the financial resources of the union, better to withstand an interruption of his employment. But it may also be realized by shifting the indifference system of one's partner by rendering it more difficult for him to dispense with the contract.

Thus, we see the connection between the theory of bilateral monopoly and our analysis of the influence-effect of foreign trade. The shifting of the indifference systems, however, has been considered until now only as a means toward the attainment of a better bargain.

---

[36] That changes in bargaining power in the traditional sense are much less important than changes in bargaining power which are the outcome of changes in indifference maps has been pointed out recently in connection with wage theory by J. T. Dunlop and Benjamin Higgins, "Bargaining Power and Market Structures," *Journal of Political Economy*, Vol. L (February, 1942), pp. 4–5.

In our analysis the possibility of driving a better bargain was only incidental to the main aim, which consisted of tying the trading partner to a country using foreign trade for purposes of national power. We have shown how this may be accomplished:

1) with an unchanged indifference system of the trading partner, by making him better off, i.e., by granting him better terms of trade;

2) with an unchanged total level of satisfaction of the trading partner, by changing his indifference system so as to make him worse off in the eventuality of interruption of trade.[37]

Because we have seen that the first solution would conflict with the supply effect of foreign trade, we have therefore mainly dwelt upon the second solution. Our analysis has thus led us to drop two of the basic assumptions of the theory of bilateral monopoly:

1) that we are in the presence of fixed indifference systems;

2) "that the one exchanger is insulated from the other in the sense that his economic conduct is not influenced in any way by the satisfaction which he conceives to be obtained by his correspondent."[38]

But in our problem, A is vitally concerned about B's satisfaction, for, by such concern, B's dependence on A is increased and the increase of satisfaction of B is brought about mainly by a change of B's indifference system. The difficulty of shifting trade to a third country may readily be taken account of in the construction of these indifference systems. The no-gain-from-trade curve of B becomes then a *no-gain-from-trade-with-A* curve, i.e., expresses the various bargains at which it would barely pay B to shift its trade with A to a third country. This curve will generally express a higher level of satisfaction of B than the ordinary no-gain-from-trade curve, but will coincide with it if no substitution is possible.

All our analysis of the influence effect of foreign trade may then be summarized by the following principle: Given a certain gain from trade of A and a fixed indifference system of A, create conditions such as to maximize the difference in satisfaction between the

---

[37] In the first case, the trading partner arrives at a higher indifference curve and the level of satisfaction expressed by the no-gain-from-trade curve remains the same; in the second case, the trading partner remains at the same indifference curve, but the no-gain-from-trade curve expresses a lower level of satisfaction than before. In both cases, his gain from trade increases, either because he actually gains more by the trade or because he would stand to lose more from a stoppage of trade.

[38] Pigou, *op. cit.*, p. 207.

indifference curve which B actually reaches by trading with A and B's no-gain-from-trade-with-A curve.

As we shall later have occasion to point out (p. 79), an economic system guided by the objective of welfare must also provide for and organize the use of economic power. At present we see that the "economics of power" may use welfare analysis to great advantage. And moralists may well ponder over the fact that concern about the trading partner's satisfaction becomes relevant for economic analysis when it is considered as a step toward eventual domination.

A NOTE ON GAIN FROM TRADE

We shall be concerned here with the relation of the welfare gain to some objective measures or indicators of the gain from trade. Our first point will be to prove that under the simplest assumptions a subjective gain from trade is possible without any specialization upon opening of trade, i.e., without any increase of aggregate production of the two countries. Because it is possible to simplify the diagrammatical exposition, we shall now use the common indifference map. Under the assumption of similar tastes in the two countries, the diagram need represent only one system of indifference curves.[39] In accordance with other assumptions which have been seen to be implicit in classical theory,[40] we shall suppose in addition that the two products exchanged are of equal importance. This somewhat imprecise concept may be defined in the following way: The income elasticity for both commodities is unity throughout the indifference map and, if the terms of exchange are fixed so that a unit of the one commodity exchanges against one unit of the other commodity, then, whatever the real income, expenditure will be divided equally between the two commodities. These assumptions yield an indifference map which is entirely symmetrical with respect

[39] Cf., in particular, the models given by W. W. Leontief, "The Use of Indifference Curves in the Analysis of Foreign Trade," *Quarterly Journal of Economics*, Vol. XLVII (May, 1933), pp. 493–503. The objections to this method, as formulated by Professor Viner (*op. cit.*, pp. 521 ff.), could be taken account of partly by interpreting the indifference curves of the community so as to include in their shape, not only the satisfaction derived from the consumption of the commodities, but, in addition, the satisfaction derived from their production. As to the meaningfulness of the concept "community indifference curves," see Kaldor, *op. cit.*, pp. 377–378, and De Scitovsky, *op. cit.*, pp. 89–95.

[40] Cf. F. D. Graham, "The Theory of International Values Reëxamined," *Quarterly Journal of Economics*, Vol. XXXVIII (November, 1923), pp. 56 ff.

to the two coördinates. Let us assume also that each of two countries of equal size has its own constant costs levels, but that these levels, as between the two, are different. For our purposes the concept "countries of equal size" means that country A can produce in complete specialization either x units of commodity a, or y units of b,

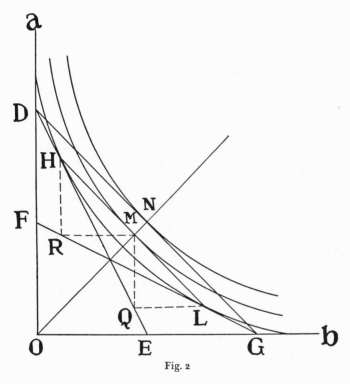

Fig. 2

whereas country B can produce y units of a, or x units of b. These assumptions are graphically presented in figure 2, in which the abscissa represents the amounts of commodity a, and the coördinate the amounts of commodity b. The curves are indifference curves common to both countries. DE is the substitution line of country A enjoying a comparative advantage in production of commodity a. FG is the substitution line of country B. They are straight lines because of our assumption of constant costs. Then, with no trade, the equilibrium for each country will be established at points H and L, at which an indifference curve touches the respective substitution lines. If trade now opens and specialization does not yet set in, both countries can move to a point M lying on a higher indifference curve—country A by exchanging RH of a for RM of b, and country B by exchanging QL (= RM) of b for QM (= RH) of a. If A specializes in the production of a, and B in the production of b, they can of course get to a point N lying on a still higher indifference curve.

In our graph the two countries start from the same indifference curve, and by trade reach a higher indifference curve common to them (either at M or at N). The assumptions through which we have obtained an equal gain from trade for both countries are extremely rigid and unrealistic. It is sufficient to drop one of these assumptions in order to obtain different welfare-gains for both countries.

If the substitution lines of countries A and B are not DE and FG, but OD and OG (A can produce only commodity a, and B only commodity b), both countries will be, in the absence of trade, at a lower level of satisfaction than in our previous case. If trade opens, they will immediately move to point N without any further specialization being possible. The volume of trade will be the same as in our previous case after specialization had taken place, but the gain from trade will be greater, as the two countries have started from lower indifference curves. Generally, the gain from trade is thought to be intimately associated with international specialization. So far as more specialization permits a greater volume of trade, this association, at least as a presumption, is warranted. But it is often forgotten that specialization is, after all, only a *pis-aller*, i.e., a course which has to be taken if the diversity of products produced in the two countries does not permit a continued profitable exchange. A presumption exists, therefore, that *with a given volume of trade* the gain from trade is the greater the *less* specialization there has been after the opening up of trade. This does not contradict established theory in any way; in fact, it is mentioned only because the connection between specialization and gain from trade is ingrained in most minds in too rigid a manner.

Short-run and long-run gain from trade and the requirements of a comprehensive theory of the gain from trade will be our next concern. The gain from trade is always the difference in satisfaction between two situations in equilibrium, the one before opening of trade or after the stoppage of trade and the other when trade is in full swing. The change in the productive structure of the country between the two points is expressed by a movement along the substitution curve. If, in figure 2, we consider the substitution line DE, and suppose that trade is suddenly interrupted, the country would revert from N to D and would then aim at point H. The short-run gain from trade is thus the difference in satisfaction between point N and point D, whereas the long-run gain from trade—the only gain which has hitherto received attention—is smaller, since it is indicated by the difference in satisfaction between point N and point H. If there is a sudden worsening of the terms of trade so that the productive structure cannot be adapted, a situation may therefore arise in which trade, while still yielding a short-run gain, results in a long-run loss. In this particular case, what is true in general about the abolition of protection holds for the stoppage of trade: It would result in immediate loss, but in ultimate benefit.

In the static theory of international trade, no account is taken of the time which is involved in changing the productive structure. The substitution curve is a long-run curve, i.e., its shape is not limited by any finite period of time, but only by the available techniques and factors of production. If we introduce time into our analysis, we see immediately that the shape of the substitution curve itself is changed. We will have two entirely different substitution curves according as we allow the period of two years or ten years for changes in the productive structure to take place.[41] This means that we have no longer a single gain from trade nor a simple subdivision into short-run and long-run gains, but a whole array of *dated* gains from trade of which the long-run and the short-run gains are the two extreme items. But all those dated gains would still relate to a given degree of employment and of utilization of resources in general. We obtain a new family of substitution curves by considering this degree of employment as a variable.

To complicate matters further, the gains thus indexed by length of adjustment time and by degree of employment are subjective in two senses: (1) because they are related to the comparison of two levels of satisfaction, and (2) because one of these levels is necessarily the result of expectations. Because of this fact the gain from

---

[41] Professor Haberler mentions the fact that the substitution curve will be more "bulged" the less the time allowed for. Cf. Haberler, *op cit.*, p. 179.

trade loses its unity for a third time; indeed, there is not only a different gain from trade for every adjustment period and level of employment contemplated, but for every single case there may be different expectations of gains. Furthermore, these expectations relate, not only to the resources within a country and to their mobility, but also to the degree to which it will be possible to draw on the resources of other countries by means of loans, immigration, etc. A comprehensive theory of the gain from trade would thus take account of the time element, of the level of employment within the country, of all types of international economical relations, and would be largely built upon a theory of expectations.

CHAPTER III

The Question of "Economic Aggression" During World War I

In the preceding chapter we have tried to show in detail why and how it is possible to turn foreign trade into an instrument of power, of pressure, and even of conquest. The Nazis have done nothing but exploit to the fullest possibilities *inherent* in foreign trade within the traditional framework of international economic relations. This is the general lesson which should emerge from the experience of economic penetration of such countries as Hungary, Bulgaria, Rumania, and other countries less successfully penetrated by "bloodless invasion." What are the conclusions which can be drawn from this experience when the present war will be won by the United Nations? Should we, because of its evil potentialities, try to limit international intercourse? Should special safeguard or boycott measures be erected against German trade once the war is over? Should we be content with prohibiting certain practices and technical devices, such as bilateral clearings, differential exchange rates, etc., which have been a prominent feature of German policies in the 'thirties? Or should we rather endeavor to build a new framework of international relations in which this use of foreign trade for purposes of national power would encounter more difficulties than hitherto? And how could this end be achieved?

Before attempting to give an answer to these momentous questions, we shall try to gain perspective by recalling how similar problems were recognized but not resolved during and after World War I.

The literature on the commercial and economic policies of Nazi Germany being rather voluminous, it is surprising not to find in it—so far as the author is aware—a single reference to the parallel and equally copious literature which was published before and during World War I. The accusations voiced against Germany at that time were in their substance very similar to those we hear today.

The intellectual level of the writings on this subject, however, compares rather unfavorably with the contemporary literature; this may be one of the reasons for which these books, like discreditable relatives, have been permitted to fall into oblivion. In addition, the *methods* by which Germany was said to achieve her end of economic conquest before World War I were different from those which she has used more recently.

The following features of German trade attracted most attention in the days before the First World War:

1) The rapid expansion of German exports, both absolutely and relatively, to other countries;

2) The scientific methods by which this expansion was achieved—in particular, the systematic study of the needs and habits of foreign consumers;

3) Unfair competition and, in particular, the dumping of some German exports. Contrary to this, the selling of potash abroad at prices higher than the home price;

4) The attempt by Germany, in connection with the dumping, to prevent industrialization in other countries and to destroy competitive industries which had already been established;

5) The export of German capital, business enterprises, and of managerial and scientific personnel;

6) German methods of financial control over foreign enterprises.

The first two points were discussed as early as the 1890's in England and France and were mooted in an intensely alarmist literature of which E. E. Williams' *Made in Germany* was the most celebrated specimen.[1] Although this literature often adopts such military figures of speech as "conquest" or "capture" of foreign markets, the danger against which it seeks to mobilize is not generally the economic or political dependence of the countries exposed to the German "trade offensive" but the lagging of British or French exports in these countries. Foreign and, in particular, export trade is viewed as an end in itself and not as a means to political penetration and economic subjugation.[2]

---

[1] For a detailed description and bibliography of the English writings, see Ross J. S. Hoffmann, *Great Britain and the German Trade Rivalry 1875–1914* (Philadelphia, 1933). The French are represented by Marcel Schwob, *Le Danger Allemand* (Paris, 1898); Georges Blondel, *L'essor industriel et commercial du peuple allemand* (Paris, 1898); Maurice Lair, *L'impérialisme allemand* (Paris, 1902).

[2] It is interesting to note that the same factual background, i.e., the rapid advance of German foreign trade, provided the subject of great anxiety, not only for England

Only at a later stage was Germany accused of consciously using her foreign economic relations as an instrument of domination. So much was still made of the German trading methods, the personal contact, the thorough study of consumers' needs, the ability of her representatives abroad to learn foreign languages, etc., that one often wonders whether the authors' purposes were one of praise for or denunciation of Germany.[3] But the emphasis shifted from these aspects of German commercial policy to the other points (3 to 6) enumerated above. The frequent dumping of German goods abroad was not seen as an instance of differential price policy practiced by a discriminating monopoly. It was supposed that dumping served a policy bent upon destroying competition in the foreign market so as to secure a monopolistic position for the German exporters and to enable them later to raise their price. This claim bears a striking similarity to the recent accusations against Germany according to which she has bought supplies at artificially high prices in other countries in order to secure there a monopsonistic position and to be able later to *lower* the prices—either directly or by manipulation of exchange rates.

No detailed study seems to exist about the question of how far German dumping before World War I was actuated by so-called "predatory" motives. According to Professor Viner, who, after the war, rendered a balanced judgment on the matter, German dumping has received far more attention than it deserves. He contends that all nations have engaged in dumping at one time or another, and, in general, he looks upon the accusations leveled against Germany on this account with some skepticism.[4] He states, however, that "there is general agreement that before 1914 export dumping was more widespread and was more systematically practised in Germany than in any other country,"[5] and "it is even probable that predatory motives were a more important factor in German dumping than in the dumping of other countries." In particular, a "well substantiated and important instance of dumping with a deliberate

---

and France, fearful of German competition, but also for Germany, apprehensive of her increasing dependence on foreign countries. (See below, pp. 146 ff.)

[3] See, e.g., P. P. Gourvitch, *How Germany Does Business* (New York, 1917). This little book gives some interesting examples of the German trading methods in Russia.

[4] Jacob Viner, *Dumping: A Problem of International Trade* (Chicago, 1924), p. 52.

[5] *Ibid.*, p. 51.

intent of crushing the domestic industry in the market dumped on is to be recorded against the Stahlwerksverband in its export policy with respect to Italy."[6]

Of course, as soon as one interprets dumping as an attempt to secure a monopolistic position in the market of a foreign country, the suspicion of an "ultra-economic" motive of domination follows almost automatically.

Another feature in German external economic policies which led to this suspicion was the export of German enterprises and scientific personnel and the penetration of German capital into foreign enterprise. The most vigorous book on this subject was published in Italy by G. Preziosi under the impressive title, *Germany Poised to Conquer Italy.*[7] The ownership and operation by a group of German bankers of the Banca Commerciale Italiana provided the central point of this book, which was widely read and aroused much interest at the time. It pictured with a good deal of exaggeration, but the more vividly, the disastrous consequences of the control by Germany of Italy's most important commercial bank, which, on the pattern of German banks, carried on an extensive financing business. According to Preziosi, Germany did her best to prevent the industrialization of Italy and, where this was impossible, she sought to obtain by financial devices the control of Italy's key industries—textile, metallurgical, and shipping. In addition, the Banca Commerciale, which had "its arms in Italy but its head in Berlin,"[8] favored German trade by all kinds of stratagems and invested Italian savings abroad in enterprises controlled by Germany. Preziosi accuses the Germans of industrial espionage and the Banca Commerciale of stopping credit facilities to firms which show an anti-German attitude. He points out cases of open or veiled political corruption and suspects the hand of Germany in industrial strikes, employing for all these activities of the Banca Commerciale the familiar term, "the Trojan Horse."

In general, Preziosi has this to say about German methods:

Pan-Germanism acts everywhere applying always the same rational and well studied procedure, which consists in the foundation of one or sev-

---

[6] *Ibid.*, p. 64. Bibliography concerning this case of dumping is given there.

[7] Giovanni Preziosi, *La Germania alla conquista dell'Italia* (Florence, 1914), introduction by Maffeo Pantaleoni, the well-known economist; I am referring to the second, the 1916, edition.   [8] *Ibid.*, p. 11.

eral banks, in the capture thereby of the credit system, of savings, trade, industry, and the merchant marine, and in the creation of a dense network of interests and customers—with the result of rendering other nations subservient to Germany.[9]

If Preziosi wrote the most sensational book on the methods of German economic penetration before the First World War, the most detailed and authoritative statement on the same subject is that of the French historian Henri Hauser.[10] His book, written in 1915, is wholly dedicated to the proposition that "economic war, conquest of markets,—words applied to Germany—are not at all metaphors. More than ever we have the feeling that Germany made war in the midst of peace with the instruments of peace. Dumping, export subsidies, import certificates, measures with respect to emigration, etc., all these various methods were used not as normal methods of economic activity, but as means to suffocate, to crush, and to terrorize Germany's adversaries."[11]

Having described these methods in detail with special emphasis on dumping and on the export of capital as practiced by Germany, he concludes: "By this concentration of all its energies, by this unity of direction, economic Germany has become a power at least as formidable as military Germany and of the same order: a power of domination and of conquest."[12]

It would be easy to add to these quotations examples from other authors.[13] It is not our task here to examine how much truth there was in the accusations of Preziosi, Hauser, and others, and how far the foreign economic policies of Imperial Germany had been centrally and systematically planned in advance with the "ultra-

[9] *Ibid.*, p. 35.
[10] Henri Hauser, *Les méthodes allemandes d'expansion économique* (Paris, 1915), (English translation, *Germany's Commercial Grip on the World* [New York, 1917]).
[11] *Ibid.*, 8th ed. (Paris, 1919), p. 4.
[12] *Ibid.*, pp. 258–259.
[13] E.g., Maurice Millioud, *The Ruling Caste and Frenzied Trade in Germany*, translated from the French (Boston, 1916); Henri Lichtenberger and Paul Petit, *L'impérialisme économique allemand* (Paris, 1918); Siegfried Herzog, *The Future of German Industrial Exports* (New York, 1918); also see below, p. 60. For factual surveys, cf. U. S. Bureau of Foreign and Domestic Commerce, *German Foreign Trade Organization* (Washington, 1917), and *German Trade and the War* (Washington, 1918). An interesting study in national self-criticism, which tries to explain the reasons for world-wide suspicion and hatred against Germany in general and German trade in particular, was given by the philosopher, Max Scheler, *Die Ursachen des Deutschenhasses* (Leipzig, 1917).

economic" aim of domination and eventual conquest. In the main, these writings were tracts which added the economic aspect to the literature on Germany's diplomatic preparations for war. They give only one side of the picture, forgetting that foreign trade and export of capital implied also a dependence of Germany on other nations; in general they were entirely lacking in systematic analysis of the connection between national power and international economic relations.

This much is certain: The possibility of using external economic relations for purposes of power policy was clearly recognized; whatever its objective foundation in economic history or theoretical analysis, it had become a very strong subjective reality. For many persons it turned into an obsession, people always being prone to believe both that they are being maneuvered by hidden forces and that the worst has been prevented just at the last moment. Thus, Briand, then French Prime Minister, declared at the opening of the Paris Economic Conference of the Allies in 1916: "The war has opened our eyes to the peril; it has abundantly demonstrated the economic slavery into which the enemy sought to drag us; we must recognize that . . . our adversaries came very near to success."[14] Similarly, Mr. Hughes, Australian Prime Minister, issued a statement after the conference in which he said: "Some Allies were before the War so completely enmeshed in the toils of Germany that they had lost all but the shadow of their nationality, and even now they are obsessed with the fear that peace will find them again in the grip of the enemy."[15] It was indeed at this very conference that the anxieties of a possible renewal of "silent economic penetration" after the war found an official expression of far-reaching importance. Anxieties of this sort had been intensified during the war by German projects for Mitteleuropa and by persistent reports that German warehouses were overflowing with goods intended for a trade offensive immediately upon the cessation of hostilities.

Let us now inquire how political leaders and economists reacted to the discovery that foreign economic relations could be, had been, and probably would again be used as an instrument of national power policy. How was the danger to be averted? In other words,

[14] *Le Temps*, June 15, 1916.
[15] *Times* (London), June 21, 1916.

how did the experience affect thinking on postwar economic reconstruction and thus postwar economic policy?

In the main, it is possible to distinguish two schools of thought.
The writers who had aroused the public to the danger of "silent
economic penetration" were ardent advocates of preparing defensive or offensive weapons from the arsenal of economic nationalism.
Aligned against them were the defenders of the virtues of free trade
who ignored or denied the danger to which their adversaries had
pointed.

It was only too easy to exploit the possibility of "economic aggression" by sovereign nations as an argument against free commercial
intercourse. The demand for increased protection seemed to be
much more compelling and much less oriented toward mere vested
interests if the evil portrayed by the protectionist was economic
aggression and penetration rather than foreign competition. The
necessity of revision of accepted thinking on free trade and protection in favor of the latter was emphasized by Hauser, who declared
that "no theory can prevail over the facts."[16] The same note was
struck by Briand in his already-quoted speech at the Paris Economic
Conference: "You will be less attentive to the traditional theoretical
doctrines and to old customs than to the new realities which are
imposing themselves upon us. If it is proved that old errors have
almost permitted our enemies to establish an irretrievable tyranny
over the productive forces of the world, you will abandon these
errors and enter new roads." And the London *Times* was in happy
agreement with "the truth that the economic situation arising out
of the war and the problems attending it cannot be dealt with by
muttering any shibboleth."[17]

The universal endorsement of "realism," as against theories and
abstractions considered as "shibboleth," is an aspect of what Benda
was to describe after the First World War as the intellectual victory
of Germany.[18] This victory went even so far that some of the very
authors who denounced German commercial methods had nothing
better to propose than to use these methods on behalf of their own
countries and for the very aims for which Germany had used them.

---

[16] Hauser, *op. cit.* p. iv.
[17] *Times* (London), June 23, 1916, editorial.
[18] Julien Benda, *La trahison des clercs* (Paris, 1927), p. 72.

Thus, Preziosi wanted to build up strong Italian industries so that they may "in their own time practice dumping, turning against the Germans their own favorite weapons."[19] Similarly, he wished to free the Banca Commerciale from German influence because "the banking system has to be one of the most powerful instruments which the state has at its disposal in order to direct international policy according to its own aims."[20] Thus, it is not surprising to be informed by the *Enciclopedia Italiana* that Preziosi early joined the Fascist party and had an important part in the elaboration of its economic program before the march on Rome.

In a more balanced fashion, Hauser made a distinction in his final chapter between "what we shall not imitate from Germany" and "what we shall have to imitate." This shows rather significantly the way in which the whole problem was raised. But in spite of his moderate position—he rejected the more aggressive German methods, such as dumping, and did not favor a complete boycott of Germany after the war's end—he advocated an "economic offensive" even after the war as the only possible answer to German methods.[21]

These instances suffice to show the general features of a current of thought which received its practical expression and official consecration at the Paris Economic Conference. This was, significantly, the only Allied conference during the war at which problems of postwar economic reconstruction were under consideration. A short survey of its resolutions and its influence upon later events seems therefore to be warranted.[22]

The resolutions adopted by six Allied nations—England, France, Italy, Russia, Belgium, Japan—fell into three parts: measures for the war period; measures for the transition period after the war; and permanent measures. The aim of the conference is clearly stated in the preamble to the resolutions:

The representatives of the Allied governments . . . declare that, after forcing upon them the military contest in spite of all the efforts to avoid the conflict, the Empires of Central Europe are today preparing, in concert with their allies, for a contest on the economic plane, which will not

[19] Preziosi, *op. cit.*, p. 43.
[20] Preziosi, *op. cit.*, p. 58.
[21] Hauser, *op. cit.*, p. ix.
[22] For a history of the genesis of the conference, see Etienne Clémentel, *La France et la Politique Economique Interalliée* (Paris–New Haven, 1931), pp. 74–78.

only survive the reëstablishment of peace, but will at that moment attain its full scope and intensity.

They cannot therefore conceal from themselves that the agreements which are being prepared for this purpose between their enemies have the obvious object of establishing the domination of the latter over the production and the markets of the whole world and of imposing .on other countries an intolerable yoke.

In the face of so great a peril, the representatives of the Allied governments consider that it has become their duty, on grounds of necessary and legitimate defense, to adopt and realize from now onward all the measures requisite on the one hand to secure for themselves and for the whole of the markets of neutral countries full economic independence and respect for sound commercial practice and, on the other hand, to facilitate the organization on a permanent basis of their economic alliance.[23]

In this preamble the spirit which dominated the conference becomes clear. The economic sovereignty, even of the defeated enemy, is not questioned, and it is supposed that economic war will continue after the end of military war. Under this assumption the main preoccupation of the Allies became "economic defense," which is very often indistinguishable from economic warfare.[24]

We are interested here in the resolutions of the conference only so far as they deal with the transition period or with the permanent arrangements after the war. These sections, reproduced in Appendix B, should be read in their entirety. Indeed, they make familiar reading.

One after another we find enumerated all the fundamental policies of refined economic nationalism with which we have become so well acquainted in the period between the two wars—restricted access to raw materials and resources, preferential treatments and discriminations, restrictions on the activities of aliens, antidumping legislation, differential transport rates, autarky, not only with respect to key industries, but on a practically universal scale by means

---

[23] Quoted from H. W. V. Temperley, *A History of the Peace Conference of Paris,* Vol. V (London, 1921), p. 367.

[24] *Le Temps* had a somewhat lukewarm attitude toward the conference and showed the absurdity of this position even from a nationalistic point of view. "We think that the main economic task of the Conference is not to elaborate this modest reply to a project which is assumed to be already realized, but on the contrary by all means to prevent the realization of this project and the formation of this Mitteleuropa, although some persons apparently would like to confine themselves to preparing a shield against its blows."—*Le Temps,* June 15, 1916.

of subsidies, tariffs, prohibitions, etc. Even a cursory view of this amazing Pandora's box raises doubts whether these measures were devised for defense only.

The Paris Resolutions were to be considered as a basic program. Each of the Allies promised to work out its own program in terms of national policies. Each, furthermore, was to be informed of the program decisions of the other. The agreement had not been reached easily. The French and English delegations met with some resistance from the Russian and Italian delegations. Before the war the two latter countries had relied heavily on the German market and viewed with some apprehension the possibilities of German reprisals. The Russian delegates opposed the period of five years which had been proposed by the English delegation as the minimum period during which Germany was to be excluded from most-favored-nation treatment; Russia obtained the much vaguer wording "for a number of years to be fixed by mutual agreement."[25]

The Russian government, however, was mainly fearful lest too intimate an understanding with the Allies on postwar economic policy might, by the establishment of conventional tariffs, restrict Russia's contemplated full use of economic sovereignty. This is evident from the governmental instruction to the delegates, which underlined "the necessity of a thorough-going, unhindered development of our productive forces and organization on as large a scale as will be practicable of our vast natural resources. . . . In order to avoid the enslavement of our industry by foreign enterprises and to make it absolutely independent we must, as a just measure, create autonomous tariffs, where the tariff on goods is not fixed by agreement with individual countries but is established by legislative chambers in accordance with the needs of the country, leaving us complete freedom to alter the tariffs in order to protect whatever branch of national industry may need it."[26] As we see, such opposition as existed within the conference against the Anglo-French proposals was motivated by the fear that the prospected policy did not go far *enough* in the direction of economic nationalism. What Russia really objected to was not discrimination against Germany

[25] Baron Boris E. Nolde, *Russia in the Economic War* (New Haven, 1928), pp. 167–168.

[26] Quoted in Nolde, *op. cit.*, p. 163.

as much as it was postwar economic collaboration between Germany and Russia's wartime Allies.

Although less evident on the surface, a similar tendency was noticeable in Great Britain, where the emphasis shifted slowly from Allied economic solidarity against the enemy to British protection against the foreigner and to the problem of imperial supply.[27]

One of the driving spirits behind the British delegation was, indeed, W. A. S. Hewins, a prominent tariff reformer and imperialist.[28] Seeing in the Paris Resolutions a powerful lever for eventually achieving tariff protection and imperial preference, he attributed to them an enormous and beneficial importance; this, in spite of the harmful effects felt from them in the midst of the war.

The resolutions, indeed, lent substance to the German claim that England had engineered and entered the war out of jealousy for German trade;[29] and Lloyd George himself pointed out later to Hewins that they had prolonged the war by drawing the German people closer together, impressed by the fear of economic strangulation after the war.[30] Again, the resolutions caused strong misgivings in neutral countries and, in particular, momentarily estranged the United States. Thus we read in Baker's *Woodrow Wilson, Life and Letters:*

When confidential telegrams brought reports of the agreements being negotiated at the Paris Economic Conference, June 14th to June 17th, the State Department became exceedingly apprehensive. The more Lansing thought about the matter, the more positive he was that the Allies were deliberately making encroachments upon the rights of neutrals under the guise of measures against Germany. He warned the President June 23 that the results of the Paris pacts might be "very far-reaching on the commerce and trade of the whole world after the war is over." "The drastic measures of the Allies purpose to prevent as far as possible the rebuilding of industries and commerce (of the Central Powers) after the war . . . the knowledge of this intention to continue the war industrially . . . will cause the Central Powers to hesitate in taking steps toward a restoration of peace. . . . In view of these possibilities would it not be

---

[27] W. K. Hancock, *Survey of British Commonwealth Affairs*, Vol. II, Part I (London, 1940), p. 96.

[28] Hancock, *op. cit.*, p. 138; W. A. S. Hewins, *The Apologia of an Imperialist* (mostly in diary form), Vol. II (London, 1929), *passim.*

[29] Alfred Marshall, "National Taxation after the War," in *After-War Problems*, ed. by W. W. Dawson (London, 1917), p. 344.

[30] Hewins, *op. cit.*, p. 132–133.

well to consider the advisability of holding a Congress of Neutrals to ... determine upon ways and means to relieve the present situation and to provide for the future ... the best way to fight combination is combination"?

The same fears cropped out in a Senate resolution ... inquiring of the President what was the "character, form and full purpose of this new action by the Allies."[31]

The Paris Resolutions were submitted in England in July, 1916, "for special reference" to a newly appointed "Committee on Commercial and Industrial Policy After the War." The chairman of this committee was Lord Balfour of Burleigh, and Mr. Hewins was one of its members. The committee's final report is dated December 3, 1917, i.e., eight months after the entry of the United States into the war. At that time the world-wide extension of the Entente, together with the *letter* of the Paris Resolutions which, after all, had foreseen a postwar economic alliance between the Entente countries, could have led to the planning of a strong nucleus for future international economic collaboration. But it was the nationalistic and restrictionist *spirit* of the Paris Conference which prevailed. In spite of a number of qualifications the emphasis of the Balfour Committee's report is on imperial preference, postwar restrictions of trade with former enemy countries, protection of essential industries, protection against dumping and "sweated goods," control of economic activities exercised by aliens, and, finally, the rejection of the decimal system in weights, measures, and coinage!

Only three months earlier, President Wilson had already foreshadowed his own program of postwar economic reconstruction in the American reply to the Pope's offer of mediation:

Responsible statesmen must now everywhere see, if they never saw before, that no peace can rest securely upon political or economic restrictions meant to benefit some nations and cripple or embarrass others, upon vindictive action of any sort, or any kind of revenge or deliberate injury. ... Punitive damages, the dismemberment of empires, the establishment of selfish and exclusive economic leagues we deem inexpedient and, in the end, worse than futile, no proper basis for a peace of any kind, least of all for an enduring peace.[32]

---

[31] Ray Stannard Baker, *Woodrow Wilson, Life and Letters,* Vol. VI (New York, 1937), pp. 229–230.

[32] *New York Times,* August 29, 1917. In the original draft of his reply, the President had used the word "childish" instead of "inexpedient." In deference to Allied senti-

In addition to his position on grounds of principle, Wilson repeatedly pointed out how impolitic it was to menace Germany with punitive measures against her trade after the war, since such threats would inevitably stiffen the German spirit of resistance.[33]

Thus, a clear-cut opposition is obvious between the spirit of the Paris Resolutions and the Balfour Committee's report, on the one hand, and the policy of the American President, on the other.[34] This opposition remained unresolved and was brought into the open one year later at Versailles.

The kernel of the economic reconstruction after the First World War should have been the third of Wilson's Fourteen Points, which called for "the removal, so far as possible, of all economic barriers and the establishment of an equality of trade conditions among all the nations consenting to the peace, and associating themselves for its maintenance." But two months before the Armistice, Clémentel, the French wartime Minister of Commerce, who in 1915 had initiated the Paris Economic Conference, addressed a detailed letter to Clémenceau and Wilson outlining the French program of postwar economic organization.[35] This program was directly inspired by the Paris Resolutions, being an ardent plea for close postwar economic collaboration among the Allies and for discriminating measures and safeguards against Germany.

Actually, Allyn A. Young, with his firsthand knowledge as the Economic Adviser to the American Peace Commission, was later to describe the third of Wilson's Fourteen Points and the Paris Resolutions as the two conflicting fountainheads of the economic

---

ment and upon the advice of Colonel House, he substituted the latter term. Cf. Charles Seymour, *The Intimate Papers of Colonel House,* Vol. III (New York, 1928) p. 164.

[33] Cf., e.g., Baker, *op. cit.,* Vol. VII, pp. 341–342.

[34] American opinion and policy, however, was not free from the influences which had shaped the Paris Resolutions. A publication of the Bureau of Foreign and Domestic Commerce on *German Trade and the War* (Washington, 1918) quotes approvingly in its conclusion a speech by an Italian industrialist, from which we extract the following characteristic passage: "The German people, feeling the bitter lesson of their defeat, will renounce, let us hope, for a long time, their mad ideas of reconquest or of revenge, but it will be necessary in every way for us to make haste in defense against their methods of economic invasion."—*Op. cit.,* p. 153. Cf. also the introduction, by Herbert Hoover, Vernon Kellogg, and Frederick C. Walcott, in the book by Siegfried Herzog quoted above. The most violent book on the German economic menace known to the present writer was written *after the end of the war* by an American journalist, Stanley Frost, under the title, *Germany's New War Against America* (New York, 1919).

[35] Clémentel, *op. cit.,* pp. 337–348.

sections of the treaty.[36] The real nature of the compromise is, however, visible in articles 264 and 265, which impose most-favored-nation treatment upon Germany without stipulating anything with respect to the commercial policy of the Allies. According to the Paris Resolutions, the Allies should have refused most-favored-nation treatment to Germany "for a number of years," whereas, according to Wilson's Third Point, they should obviously have granted her "equality of trading conditions." The silence concerning the commercial policy of the Allies meant that there was no open contradiction between the treaty and Wilson's Third Point, but that in practice the door was open for the application of the Paris Resolutions. It was also in the spirit of the Paris Conference to act as if the political independence of the restored or newly created nations could be nothing but a "sham independence" unless supplemented by full "economic independence," which not only meant full economic sovereignty but even implied efforts to be self-sufficient with regard to all essential economic activities.

The system proposed by Wilson was based upon the relatively liberal policies—reducing trade barriers and supporting nondiscrimination—to be conducted independently by the various nations retaining, in all other respects, their full economic sovereignty. But the Paris Resolutions had outlined a restrictionist and discriminating policy which was to be implemented by an enduring association of the Allied powers even after the war. Between these two poles, the economic groundwork laid at Versailles and the commercial and economic policies worked out during the pre-1939 peace years, a compromise of the worst kind was evolved, combining as it did the principle of full economic sovereignty and the practices of restriction and discrimination.

With that refined instinct which can only be created by passionate partisanship, Hewins detected the intrinsic weakness of the Wilsonian position as early as 1917. Commenting on Wilson's reply to the Pope's offer of mediation, Hewins asserted what was to become

---

[36] Allyn A. Young, "The Economic Settlement," in *What Really Happened at Paris,* ed. by Colonel E. M. House (New York, 1921), pp. 309–317; cf. also the same author on "Commercial Policy in German, Austrian, Hungarian and Bulgarian Treaties," in *A History of the Peace Conference of Paris,* ed. by H. W. V. Temperley, Vol. V (London, 1921), p. 65, and Bernard M. Baruch, *The Making of the Reparation and the Economic Sections of the Treaty* (New York, 1930), p. 82.

the standard argument against American commercial policy: "In effect Wilson invites the Powers to adopt a policy of international free trade to protect the isolation of the U. S. A."[37] Since that time much has been said about the failure of the United States after 1918 to adjust the structure of its foreign trade to its new position as a creditor nation. And it is certainly true that the United States, constituting an immense and highly protected economic empire, was in an unfavorable position to combat "the establishment of selfish and exclusive economic leagues." Wilson himself, when pressed to comment on the third of his Fourteen Points, interpreted it in a limited sense by saying that he insisted only upon the policy of nondiscrimination. He declined to make any reference whatever to the "removal, as far as possible, of all economic barriers."[38]

The unwillingness of the United States to make a contribution to the rehabilitation of international economic relations by tariff reductions or, at least, by an agreement to stabilize existing tariffs, however, can be considered as only one reason for the utopian flavor and the eventual defeat of Wilson's policy. An even more important factor contributing to the weakness of the American—or rather, Wilsonian—position has been pointed out more recently. This was the premature breaking up of the agencies of Allied economic collaboration which had been created for war purposes but which could have been turned to the tasks of relief and reconstruction.[39]

A third element which made for the victory of economic nationalism in the period between the two wars was an insufficient appreciation of the very earnest motives which had led to the adoption of the Paris Resolutions. In describing these motives in detail, we have seen how events before 1914, how German plans for Mitteleuropa during the war, and how a body of writings on these subjects had imbued public and statesmen alike with the fear that external economic relations might be used as instruments of power policy. Not only Germany, which had gone through the experience of Allied

---

[37] Hewins, *op. cit.*, Vol. II, p. 165.

[38] Baker, *op. cit.*, Vol. VIII, pp. 503–504, 524–525. Cf., also, Seymour, *op. cit.*, Vol. IV, pp. 193–194.

[39] Cf. J. B. Condliffe, *Agenda for a Post-War World* (New York, 1942), pp. 58 f., and E. H. Carr, *Conditions of Peace* (New York, 1942), pp. 249 f. For detailed reference, see Henry B. Brodie and Karl W. Kapp, "The Breakdown of Inter-Allied Economic Collaboration in 1919," *in* National Planning Association, *United States' Coöperation with British Nations*, Planning Pamphlets, No. 6 (August, 1941).

economic blockade, but all nations had become conscious and afraid of the possibilities of economic domination. This consciousness and this fear—carefully nourished and exploited by a host of sectional interests—were to determine their external economic policy just as their internal policy was vitally affected by the Russian Revolution, which had rendered the middle classes the world over conscious and fearful of social revolution.

A considerable amount of opposition to the Paris Resolutions was evident in all the Allied countries, particularly in England and the United States; but this opposition, although fully aware of the dangerous economic and political consequences involved, generally ignored or denied the problem which the Paris Resolutions had at least attempted to solve. Let us summarize briefly this section of opinion, which formed the ideological background of President Wilson's position.

The Paris Resolutions were generally interpreted by their opponents as a wartime offensive of the protectionists; critical appraisal was often restricted to a mere restatement of the merits of free trade, of the most-favored-nation clause, and of the open-door principle.[40]

At the times it was touched upon, the idea that the state could use commercial relations for ends of national power was entirely dismissed. As early as 1904 William Smart struck this note in a book directed against the tariff reformers: "All the nonsense one hears about dumping as a 'national conspiracy' is derived from the fallacious idea which thinks of another nation as an industrial unit."[41] Still more outspoken was J. A. Hobson, who devoted a booklet to the refutation of the thesis adopted at the Paris Economic Conference.[42] In the chapter entitled "How to Meet Trade Aggression," he writes:

The German State had a powerful secret service in many foreign countries, and may have utilized branches of German firms abroad as sources of political information. The widespread employment of German clerks in foreign commercial houses has undoubtedly given German firms a fuller knowledge of the business conditions of their foreign com-

[40] *The Economist* of July 8, 1916, p. 55, reproduced in full a letter of protest by liberal peers and Members of Parliament. For a general review of the opposition in various countries, cf. E. M. Friedmann, *International Commerce and Reconstruction* (New York, 1920), pp. 108–116.

[41] William Smart, *The Return to Protection* (London, 1904), p. 161, quoted in Viner, *Dumping*, etc., *op. cit.*, p. 61.

[42] J. A. Hobson, *The New Protectionism* (New York, 1916).

petitors than commercial firms in England possess. But all these arts and practices are nothing else than an intelligent seizure of legitimate business opportunities. . . . The notion that all this expanding trade and finance have been the cat's-paw of the aggressive German state is baseless. . . . The suggestion that German traders, bankers, colonists, are merely advance agents of the German state is one of those impositions upon credulity which would not have been possible in any other atmosphere than that of war.[43]

This startling statement was written when several international crises and wars leading up to the First World War had occurred, crises in which, as future research was to show, trade and finance had often been more the instruments than the determinants of diplomacy.[44]

Even Professor Cannan, who had so clear a view of the necessities of effective international government, saw in the "new protectionism" "nothing but the old protectionism utilizing the ill-feeling created by the war and its unchivalrous incidents."[45]

Of prominent free trade economists at the time of the First World War, Edgeworth alone seems to have recognized the existence and the importance of the problem. This may be an outcome of his close contact with Continental thinking, on the one hand, and of his preoccupation with the theory of the terms of trade, on the other.[46]

He clearly recognized and, to some extent, defended "the motives of those free traders who took part in the Conference of Paris. The danger which they had in view was not the bogey of the common protectionist, not the action of normally competing merchants, but 'dumping' or some other form of 'penetration' engineered and subsidized by a hostile government acting in monopolistic fashion, like a trust when it 'freezes out' its rivals."[47] It should be noted that Edgeworth pleaded here only for a better appraisal of the *motives* of those responsible for the Paris Resolutions, not for the resolutions themselves. He was far from agreeing with them, but he recognized

[43] Hobson, *op. cit.*, pp. 78–79.

[44] Cf. Eugene Staley, *War and the Private Investor* (New York, 1935), *passim*.

[45] In the review of Mr. Hobson's book reprinted in *An Economist's Protest* (London, 1927), p. 89. Cf. also his blunt statement: "Of all the discreditable tomfooleries of which we have been the victims, the 'war on German trade' was the most idiotic."—*Ibid.*, p. 63.

[46] See above, p. 11.

[47] F. Y. Edgeworth, *Papers Relating to Political Economy*, Vol. III (London, 1925), p. 225.

clearly the reality of the question raised by him in a not unfavorable review of Preziosi's book: "How are we to define the arts and aims to which the odious character of 'conquest' is properly attributable from a 'penetration' which is really peaceful and conducive to the increase of the world's wealth and the survival of the economically fit?"[48]

Edgeworth thus stands between the two groups which our analysis of World War I discussions on postwar economic policy has revealed. Between those who ignore the danger of external economic relations becoming an instrument of national power aims and those who see the danger but try to remedy it by the defensive and offensive weapons of economic nationalism, a place should indeed be left to those who, faced with the danger, refuse to follow the policy either of the ostrich or of Gribouille.

[48] *Ibid.*, Vol. III, p. 203.

CHAPTER IV

Problems of Reconstruction

BOTH OUR THEORETICAL and historical analyses—supplemented in Part II by statistical evidence—permit certain conclusions which can be made available for the current discussion on postwar reconstruction.

The situation with which we are confronted today and which will have to be met after the end of the war is in many ways similar to that which resulted during and after World War I. As at the Paris Economic Conference of 1916 and subsequently at Versailles, the fear of "economic aggression" and the prevention of its recurrence will be a major preoccupation of our future peacemakers.

We shall examine three possible attempts to solve the question: (1) the imposition of certain restraints upon the commercial and economic policy of Germany and her allies; (2) universal free trade; and (3) the abolition of discriminating practices and the restriction of state intervention. The appraisal of these proposals will lead up to the principle which, in my opinion, should guide the reconstruction of international economic relations.

The disarmament of Germany, Italy, and Japan will certainly have to include an economic disarmament which will prevent the use of the productive powers of these countries for aggressive purposes. A distinction should, however, be made in this respect between the economic basis of military aggression and economic aggression proper. Although the task of securely preventing at the source any future rearmament of the Axis countries is admittedly a difficult one, it is not without prospect of a reasonable solution. The crucial importance of gasoline as a raw material, of the airplane as a weapon, and of the machine-tool industry as the industrial basis of modern warfare points to the possibility that a tight control in a few strategic points within a country's economy might paralyze its power to prepare for war without impairing its capacity to produce for the purposes of civilian consumption.

But the task becomes far more complicated if we turn our attention to economic aggression as a *substitute* for and complement to military aggression. Will it be sufficient to guard against it by prohibiting certain specific methods which have been prominent in the 'thirties, such as clearings, differential exchange rates, overvaluation, export subsidies, exchange dumping, and monopolization of the trade of small countries?

It follows from our previous analysis that this remedy against future economic aggression would be insufficient. In the first place, it is by no means certain that these various devices exhaust the arsenal of economic aggression. During and after World War I many countries, following the recommendations of the Paris Economic Conference, established restrictive legislation against the commercial activities of foreigners and tried to limit current capital investments. The presence of foreign personnel and capital had indeed been a prominent feature of "penetration" in the period before 1914.[1] What was the result and the effectiveness of the new regulations? Two examples may be cited: The main effect of French anti-alien legislation of 1919 was to render life difficult for refugees; and the extensive efforts of the Turkish government to get rid of foreign *capital* appear to be rather futile when it is remembered how Germany in a few years has succeeded in taking over more than half of the Turkish foreign *trade*. In shaping our future economic policy, let us not imitate the French General Staff, the mistake of which for the last eighty years has been to be always perfectly well prepared—for the last war.

There is, moreover, an overwhelming probability that nations will not put sufficient trust in the efficient working of the control over the trade of their former enemies. They will want to render impossible future attempts at economic domination, not only by restraints on Germany and her allies, but by positive action of their own. And in the framework of national sovereignties, this action spells the recrudescence of the very policy which resulted from World War I: more economic nationalism, more restriction, and more discrimination.

Here we enter a vicious circle. Restriction and discrimination undoubtedly sharpen national antagonisms. They provide also excel-

---

[1] See above, p. 55.

lent opportunities for nationalist leaders to arouse popular resentment. And if these leaders, once in power, should feel the slightest doubt concerning the best policy to adopt, they will be much encouraged in their aggressive intentions by realizing that international economic relations provide them with an excellent instrument to achieve their ends, just as a promise of a quick and crushing victory by means of aerial superiority undoubtedly contributed in a most important way to the outbreak of the present war.

How can we escape from a process of causation leading directly from one war to another? The first step toward the solution of the problem is to recognize fully its existence in all its implications. We have seen in our Chapter II how the political aspect of international trade relations arises out of the system of national sovereignties. The close interconnection of political concepts, such as "dependence on foreign countries," and of concepts of economic analysis, such as "gain from trade" or "substitute markets," has been made clear.

I do not think that the classical economists have entirely overlooked the political aspect of international economic relations. They may have given little thought to the subject, but no one has yet given a better picture of the nature of "dependence on trade" than Adam Smith, who, in his chapter on colonies, described the dangers resulting to Great Britain from her overinflated trade with the American colonies. Adam Smith, indeed, attacks Britain's colonial trade monopoly, not only on purely economic or "welfare" grounds, but also because "the whole system of her industry and commerce has thereby been rendered less secure; the whole state of her body politic less healthful than it otherwise would have been." And he continues with an analogy from the human organism, which we shall quote in full:

In her present condition, Great Britain resembles one of those unwholesome bodies in which some of the vital parts are overgrown and which, upon that account, are liable to many dangerous disorders scarce incident to those in which all the parts are more properly proportioned. A small stop in that great blood vessel, which has been artificially swelled beyond its natural dimensions, and through which an unnatural proportion of the industry and commerce of the country has been forced to circulate, is very likely to bring on the most dangerous disorders upon the whole body politic. The expectation of a rupture with the colonies, accordingly, has struck the people of Great Britain with more terror than they have ever felt for a Spanish Armada or for a French invasion. It was this terror, whether well or ill grounded which rendered the repeal of the Stamp Act a popular measure among the merchants at least. In the total exclusion from the colony market, was it to last only for a few years, the greater part of our merchants used to fancy that they foresaw an entire stop to their trade; the greater part of our master manufacturers the entire ruin of their business; and the greater part of our workmen an end of their employment. A rupture with any of our neighbors upon the continent, though likely, too, to occasion some stop or interruption in the employments of some of all these different orders of people, is foreseen, however, without any such general emotion. The blood of which the circulation is stopt in some of the smaller vessels, easily disgorges itself into the greater without occasioning any dangerous disorder; but, when it is stopt in any of the greater vessels, convulsions, apoplexy, or death, are the immediate and unavoidable consequences.[2]

Adam Smith is thus quite aware of the political dependence into which one country might fall by her trade relations; but he pictures this dependence as the consequence of an unhealthy trading system, a consequence which will disappear with the abolition of that system. He thinks that without the monopoly of the colonial trade, i.e., under free trade, there would result "a natural balance . . . among all the different branches of British industry"; trade would run "in a great number of small channels"; and there would obviously be no need to worry about the interruption of any one of these channels, as "the blood, of which the circulation is stopt in some of the smaller vessels, easily disgorges itself into the greater."[3] As we saw above, Macaulay was later to take up a very similar argument for free trade during the discussions on the Corn Laws.[4]

It seems therefore that the early English free trade economists, unlike many of their later disciples, did not ignore entirely the power aspect of international economic relations. They certainly did not simply assume the problem away by presupposing a "peaceful attitude" in men.[5] It was rather their belief that the political or power aspect of foreign trade could be *neutralized* efficiently by a universal free trade system, because the trade of every country would be so widely spread over the various markets that it need not worry

---

[2] Adam Smith, *Wealth of Nations*, p. 571.
[3] *Ibid*, pp. 570, 571.
[4] See above, p. 7.
[5] This has been contended recently by Louis Baudin, *Free Trade and Peace* (Paris, 1939), p. 26 and *passim*.

about the interruption of the trade with any particular country. Under universal free trade any country would hold only a small proportion of the total trade of any other country, and substitute markets or sources of supply would always be readily available.

Similarly, it was assumed with respect to the internal market, not that the producers would have an "attitude" opposed to the control of market price, but that any single producer would handle only so small a share of the total output that he would be *unable* to control the price of the product by altering the scale of his output. The theory of imperfect competition has shown that this situation is only very rarely realized. But the conditions which were supposed to lead to a neutralization of the power aspects of international economic relations are not merely "unrealistic," but entirely fantastic. They presuppose, indeed, a multitude of states of approximately equal importance each with approximately the same volume of foreign trade, the trade of each country being spread equally over all the other countries and no country possessing a monopoly with respect to any peculiar skill or natural endowment. In such a world there would be no special need to guard against the offensive weapons of national economic sovereignties. If universal free trade could give reality to this world, it would undoubtedly be the solution to the problem.

Actually, the division of the world into big and small, rich and poor political units combined with the fact that the poor and small countries trade but little among themselves renders this solution completely impracticable. Moreover, as we have seen in our Chapter II, so important a form of the international division of labor as that between agricultural and industrial countries leads to certain power disequilibria. The statistical analysis will show that the dependence on one or a few markets and the dependence on one or a few products are generally cumulative. In this way, foreign trade brings about a maximum degree of dependence for certain countries which is by no means always the result of conscious policy on the part of other countries.[6] A similar cumulative effect operates in the many countries which are both relatively poor and small.

It would have been easy to take the position with respect to the issue before us that we cannot wait for the reconstruction of a more

---

[6] See above, p. 13.

peaceful world until universal free trade is established. But we have not been arguing here on any such "realistic" grounds. Approximation to the free trade principle, which is by no means tied up necessarily with the institution of private enterprise,[7] remains a goal for which, despite all the difficulties of realization, it is important to strive on the grounds of economic welfare. But if the case for free trade, on economic or welfare grounds, has remained unanswerable since Adam Smith and Ricardo, our analysis shows that it does not have the additional merit of doing away with the political aspect of international economic relations.

If this is so, an argument *a fortiori* applies to the simple abolition of discriminating treatments such as quotas, preferential or discriminating duties, or exchange rates varying according to the type of transaction and the country involved. This program is much less ambitious than that of universal free trade, as, provided there is only one foreign exchange rate, it admits general tariffs and outright prohibitions as well as monetary manipulations. The most-favored-nation clause is one of the typical expressions of this system which is generally implied in such phrases as "equality of trading conditions" or "equality of trading opportunity." It was the aim of Wilson's economic reconstruction program and, so far as the reconstruction of international trade is concerned, seems still to be the only official postwar aim of the United Nations. This program is generally coupled with some attempt to limit restrictive state intervention and state trading in general.

No doubt can exist that the use of discriminatory methods as well as the power of national governments to determine directly the direction and the composition of foreign trade enables them to make the most of the power potentialities of their external economic relations. Without these methods and this power it would be difficult to enforce many of the policies which we have described in Chapter II as conducive to an increase in power. Frictions also arise very easily out of discriminating treatments and out of the identification of all private interests with the interests of the state.

But, in the first place, protectionism without discrimination is quite sufficient to increase the existing inequalities of natural and human resources and to create thereby for some nation conditions

---

[7] Cf. J. E. Meade, *The Economic Basis for a Durable Peace* (London, 1940), p. 94.

of privilege which are a factor making for an aggressive policy on the part of other nations. Secondly, every tariff implies a certain amount of discrimination against a particular country or group of countries;[8] and by skillful coördination and timing of tariffs, prohibitions, and exchange manipulations, it should be possible to obtain, with respect to the direction and the composition of trade, effects similar to those which can be reached more easily by quotas, bilateral clearings, etc. Thirdly, the "politicalization of trade" has its primary roots, as we have seen, not in the control over the flow of trade, but in the negative power of the nation-state to stop trade.[9] This power is an attribute of national sovereignty whatever may be the degree of positive state intervention. Where a possibility of using foreign trade as an instrument of national power policy exists, of course, a strong incentive is given to use this instrument in its most effective way, i.e., discrimination and state intervention. These two forms of extreme economic nationalism do not therefore appear to us to be the cause of the political aspects of international economic relations, but, rather, they appear to be their symptom and ultimate outcome.[10]

Speaking primarily of internal trade, John Stuart Mill said that

---

[8] Cf. S. H. Bailey, "The Political Aspects of Discrimination in International Economic Relations," *Economica,* Vol. XXXV (February, 1932), pp. 90–91.

[9] See above, pp. 15–17.

[10] Finally, from the economic point of view, the abolition of all types of discrimination might be both impracticable and undesirable. The term discrimination loses much of its meaning if it is applied to a state which has a centrally planned economy, the reason being that in such a state the methods of commercial policy may easily be replaced by policies relating to the internal structure of production. But even in nonplanned economies it may be extremely difficult to determine whether price differences for similar products are due to discrimination proper or to differences in the terms and conditions of the sale in two different markets. Cf., on this point, the impressive list of possible warranted price discrepancies between different markets in the Temporary National Economic Committee, Monograph No. 6, *Export Prices and Export Cartels* (Webb-Pomerene Associations), (Washington, 1940), pp. 16–28. It may also be economically *undesirable* to outlaw price discrimination which might serve welfare as well as power purposes. Price discrimination is, indeed, implicit in the numerous proposals to prolong lease-lend aid for relief and reconstruction after the war and to create even permanently a food stamp plan on an international basis. (This idea is being explored in detail in an unpublished manuscript by Dr. Peter Franck; cf. also J. B. Condliffe, *Agenda for a Post-War World* [New York, 1942], p. 113, and National Planning Association, *United States' Coöperation with British Nations,* Planning Pamphlets, No. 6, pp. 23–25.) We perceive in the difference in attitude with respect to discrimination a conflict between the political economists of liberal tradition and the economic technicians eager to avail themselves of newly discovered weapons of economic policy—a conflict which should be resolved in the interest of consistent postwar policy.

"trade is a social act.''[11] We have now reached the result that international trade remains a political act whether it takes place under a system of free trade or protection, of state trading or private enterprise, of most-favored-nation clause, or of discriminating treatments.

Still, the belief is widespread that it is possible somehow to escape this intimate connection between international trade and "power politics" and to restore trade to its "normal and beneficial economic functions." How deep-rooted this conviction is, especially in Anglo-Saxon tradition, may be seen by the famous sentence of Washington's Farewell Address: "The great rule of conduct for us, in regard to foreign nations, is, in extending our commercial relations, to have with them as little political connection as possible." It is certainly this "rule of conduct" which echoes in the mind of Douglas Miller when he renders his verdict on Nazi business methods by declaring: "We must get this straight once and for all: There is no such thing as having purely economic relations with the totalitarian states. Every business deal with them carries with it political, military, social, propaganda implications.''[12] Mr. Miller does not define "purely economic relations"; nor does he seem to suspect that, like the purely "economic man," they are an abstraction useful for economic analysis but seldom encountered in real life, especially in dealings between sovereign nations, be they totalitarian or not.

The spirit in which Mr. Miller has written is also evident when he makes a distinction, which has recently become fashionable, between the "economics of welfare" and the "economics of power" or the "economics of force." This opposition is apt to be very misleading if it implies that power relationships can be banned entirely from some ideal economic system. The distinction would be legitimate if it were intended to point out two different short-run *aims* of economic activity. But then one might better contrast the "economic *policy* of welfare" and the "economic *policy* of power."[13] The economic relationships existing in a society dedicated to the pursuit

---

[11] J. S. Mill, *On Liberty* (Boston, 1865), p. 183.

[12] Douglas Miller, *You Can't Do Business With Hitler* (New York, 1941), pp. 88–89.

[13] The dichotomy of the economics of power and of welfare has been superimposed upon the much older and neater distinction between economics of welfare and positive economics; the latter explains the working of the economic system, whereas the former is concerned with policy. This distinction was systematically developed by Edgeworth, who, in his *Mathematical Psychics*, contrasted the "economical" to the "utilitarian calculus."

of welfare inevitably give rise to various forms of economic power; and this is by no means necessarily an evil, since such a society must develop power, both political and economic, against those who do not agree with its aim of welfare. The Nazis have merely shown us the tremendous power potentialities inherent in international economic relations, just as they have given us the first practical demonstration of the powers of propaganda. It is not possible to ignore or to neutralize these relatively new powers of men over men; the only alternative open to us is to prevent their use for the purposes of war and enslavement and to make them work for our own purposes of peace and welfare.[14]

This can be done only by a frontal attack upon the institution which is at the root of the possible use of international economic relations for national power aims—the institution of national economic sovereignty.

The conclusions which we have reached are far from revolutionary. But our contribution to the increasing tide of attack against national economic sovereignty is not based merely upon the widespread opposition against the indisputable evils of economic nationalism: It proceeds even more from a frank recognition of the *risks connected with expanding trade if this trade is organized on strictly separate national lines.* Economic nationalism receives one of its main impulses from this risk, from the fear of entrusting national well-being to factors beyond the nation's control. In the present organizational and institutional setting of international trade, the choice with which we are confronted is thus quite unattractive: On the one hand, a decrease of trade due to restrictionism increases the probability of national jealousies and desires for territorial expansion; whereas, on the other hand, more commerce means greater potentialities of using trade as an instrument of military preparation, economic pressure, and blackmail. If we want to turn from the sterile alternatives between autarky and "economic penetration" to the achievement of international economic collaboration, the exclusive power to organize, regulate, and interfere with trade must be taken away from the hands of single nations. It must be trans-

---

[14] With respect to the mechanisms of social control in general, this has been pointed out convincingly by Karl Mannheim, *Man and Society in an Age of Reconstruction* (London, 1940), pp. 199–326, in particular.

ferred to an international authority able to exercise this power as a sanction against an aggressor nation.

To arrive at an internationalization of the power arising out of foreign trade, two conditions must be fulfilled:

1) The complete autonomy of national commercial policies must be effectively limited, and this limitation must cover, not only a few restricted fields of action, but the whole of international economic relations.

2) The institutional framework of foreign trade (consular services, chambers of commerce, import- and export-banks, organizations of international transportation, etc.) must be drafted on international or supranational lines. In other words, the international authority should be not only the ultimate supervisor of the machinery of international trade, but should also provide several of the most essential mechanisms of this machinery. By providing services essential to the traders, the international authority would acquire a large measure of direct control over trade. The lack of such a control was largely responsible for the inadequacy and inefficiency of Article 16 of the Covenant of the League of Nations.

It is not our task here to implement by detailed proposals these two principles. But it may be useful to stress the importance of planning in this direction. Most present postwar reconstruction schemes in the economic field seem to be inspired by the belief that the achievement of plenty and of stability constitute the necessary and sufficient condition for a lasting peace. That it is a necessary condition few would deny; and it is certainly a most encouraging feature of the present state of thought and action in this field that, although in the First World War the Allies lived in the perpetual fear of a German export offensive after the war, today the United Nations are actively preparing an offensive of food, clothing, and medical and other supplies for the populations freed from Axis control.

The elimination of violent fluctuations of economic activity and the raising of national standards of living, however essential, are only one aspect of the problem before us. Peace, it has been said, is a "virtual mute, continuous victory of the possible forces over the probable appetites."[15] Two tasks, indeed, confront the organization of peace. They are: (1) to prevent, so far as possible, the formation

---

[15] Paul Valéry, *Regards sur le monde actuel* (Paris, 1931), p. 51.

of appetites impelling to war; and (2) to weaken the forces which are at the command of such appetites while strengthening the forces by which peace can be maintained. The second task, though less fundamental than the first, remains important so long as the causes of warlike attitudes are not entirely known and extirpated.

In a rough way this task corresponds to the attainment of what President Franklin D. Roosevelt has termed "freedom from fear," whereas "freedom from want" is a preliminary condition for achieving the first objective. Most recent studies concerned with freedom from want for all peoples have put forward strong arguments against the traditional conception of national sovereignty with respect to economic policy. We have tried here to show that this conclusion is even more compelling if we are looking for ways of diminishing or abolishing fears of aggression and of penetration arising out of international trade. The internationalization of power over external economic relations would go far toward the goal of a peaceful world.

Part Two

THREE STATISTICAL INQUIRIES INTO
THE STRUCTURE OF WORLD TRADE

Three Statistical Inquiries into the Structure of World Trade

In CHAPTER II we have described the general conditions leading to greater national power by means of foreign trade. Certain of these conditions were found to have definite quantitative characteristics. It is therefore possible to test statistically the presence and evolution of these conditions, especially for the period between the two wars, excellent, easily available, and homogeneous statistics having been prepared by the League of Nations.[1]

We have undertaken three distinct inquiries, two of which concern the distribution of foreign trade with respect to countries, the third being directed to an analysis of the commodity-composition of world trade from a certain standpoint.

Examining the conditions under which country A will experience most difficulties in shifting its trade from one country B to other countries, we found that the fraction which B holds in A's total trade is an important element in evaluating the situation.[2] This fraction depends on the size of its numerator, the trade of B with A, and on the size of its denominator, A's total trade. It seems, therefore, that country B could increase its trading partners' difficulties in shifting their trade with B to other countries, either by increasing its trade with the same trading partners or by redirecting trade toward countries with a smaller total volume of trade. Our first statistical inquiry seeks, therefore, to measure the extent to which the trade of the greater trading countries is spontaneously, or has been actively, oriented toward the smaller trading countries.

If the greater trading countries have a power interest in monopolizing the trade of the smaller countries, the latter, as a defensive measure, should aim at splitting their trade equally among as many countries as possible in order to escape too great a dependence on

---

[1] *Review of World Trade* and *International Trade Statistics*.
[2] See above, pp. 30–31.

one or two great markets or supply sources. Our second statistical inquiry attempts, accordingly, to give a measure for the concentration of the trade of the smaller trading nations according to countries.

With respect to the commodity-composition of trade, we have seen that the division of labor between industrial and agricultural countries has a bearing on the power relationships between such countries. In addition, the prevention of industrialization of agricultural countries has often been founded upon the claim that such an industrialization would put an end to any "sound" international division of labor, and this view has been an important factor in shaping the economic and foreign policy of various countries. In our concluding chapter we try, therefore, to measure the extent to which world trade has actually been based in the past upon the exchange of manufactures against foodstuffs and raw materials.

So far as I am aware, the methods which have been used for the analysis of these questions are new. Since the analysis of the first two may have a more general usefulness and may require a special justification, we have attempted, in Appendix A, to fully set forth this justification. All the methods are extremely synthetic, since they attempt to summarize by a single index one special characteristic of an extended statistical series. As always, this method has its advantages and its drawbacks. The advantage lies in bringing out certain general developments which, because of the mass of the data and because of our limited powers of perception, would otherwise have remained hidden. The drawback of every synthetic method is the loss of concreteness. In other words, a movement of the index may mean many different things in terms of the original data; in order to explain adequately the difference between any two indices, one has, therefore, to go back to the original data from which the indices were computed. By the very nature of our inquiry, however, we are interested here mainly in general trends and in their comparison for various countries, or, in the third inquiry, in their computation for world trade as a whole. The indices have the function of affording a clearer perception of certain processes in the structure of world trade. We do not therefore attempt to interpret every single movement in the indices, but only those movements which seem relevant from the standpoint from which the calculation of the indices initially proceeded.

CHAPTER V

The Preference of Large Trading Countries for Commerce with Small Trading Countries

METHOD OF MEASUREMENT

IF A COUNTRY has acquired equal percentage shares in the trade of all its trading partners, it has apparently shown no preference for either large or small trading countries. In an index we have devised, 100 is the value given for this case. If the percentage shares are on the whole larger in the small trading countries, the figure rises above 100; if smaller, the figure falls below 100.

Let us suppose that country X trades with n countries the total imports and exports (including imports and exports from X) of which are represented by the symbols $I_1, I_2, \cdots, I_n$ and $E_1, E_2, \cdots, E_n$. The imports of X (or the exports of the other countries to X) are $i_1, i_2, \cdots, i_n$. Let their sum be I_x. Similarly, the exports of X are $e_1, e_2, \cdots, e_n$, and their sum is E_x. Let world exports (theoretically equal to world imports) be

$$E_w = E_1 + E_2 + \cdots + E_n + E_x{}^* = I_1 + I_2 + \cdots + I_n + I_x = I_w$$

Then, by importing from other countries, X obtains the fractions

$$\frac{i_1}{E_1}, \frac{i_2}{E_2}, \cdots, \frac{i_n}{E_n}$$

or the percentage shares

$$\frac{i_1}{E_1} \cdot 100, \frac{i_2}{E_2} \cdot 100, \cdots, \frac{i_n}{E_n} \cdot 100$$

in the total exports of these countries. We can form two arithmetic

---

* The values of the exports and the imports of the various countries are assumed to have been reduced to a common currency.

averages of the fractions or of the percentage shares, a simple average and a weighted average. The "weighted average of the (percentage) shares" is:

$$\text{W.A.} = \frac{\dfrac{i_1}{E_1} \cdot E_1 + \dfrac{i_2}{E_2} \cdot E_2 + \cdots + \dfrac{i_n}{E_n} \cdot E_n}{E_1 + E_2 + \cdots + E_n} \cdot 100$$

$$= \frac{i_1 + i_2 + \cdots + i_n}{E_1 + E_2 + \cdots + E_n} \cdot 100$$

(1) $$\text{W.A.} = \frac{I_x}{E_w - E_x} \cdot 100 = \frac{I_x}{I_w - E_x} \cdot 100$$

The "unweighted average of the shares" is:

(2) $$\text{U.A.} = \frac{1}{n} \cdot \left(\frac{i_1}{E_1} + \frac{i_2}{E_2} + \cdots + \frac{i_n}{E_n} \right) \cdot 100$$

We adopt, as index of preference of the imports of X for the smaller countries, the expression

(3) $$R = \frac{\text{U.A.}}{\text{W.A.}} \cdot 100$$

for the following reasons: The unweighted average depends upon the sum of the individual percentages secured by X in the total exports of the other countries. Every individual percentage carries the same weight whether it relates to the total trade, say, of Great Britain or of Bulgaria. The sum of the ratios secured in both these countries depends, therefore:

1) with a given distribution of X's trade as between Great Britain and Bulgaria, upon the total trade of these two countries as well as on the combined trade of X with them.

2) with given totals of Great Britain's and Bulgaria's trade and with a fixed amount of X's trade with these two countries taken together, upon the relative distribution of X's trade as between Great Britain and Bulgaria. By transferring trade from Britain to Bulgaria, X increases, indeed, the percentage secured in Bulgaria's total trade by more than it decreases the percentage held in Great Britain's total trade.

The weighted average is computed precisely to eliminate the second type of behavior of the unweighted average; it responds only to changes of the first type. It is therefore possible to isolate the factors under expression (2) by dividing the unweighted by the weighted average.

If both averages are equal, and our index consequently is equal to 100, the relative distribution of X's trade as between large and small trading countries does not exert any "distorting" effect upon the value of the unweighted average. In this case there exists, on the whole, no preference for either small or large countries. If the index rises above 100, this means that, on the whole, higher percentages are secured in the smaller trading countries; and if it falls below 100, higher percentages are secured in the larger trading countries.[1]

The calculation of the index was done by computing first the weighted and the unweighted average of the single shares held by a country's trade in the total trade of the other countries.[2] Certain definite meanings can be attached to these intermediate steps of our calculation.

Putting Germany for X, the weighted average of the percentage shares which she holds in the total exports of other countries is simply the share she occupies through her imports in the exports of all other countries lumped together. It is to be noted that this is not the quantity which is generally called "German share in world imports." This latter quantity has been calculated annually by the

---

[1] See Appendix A for a more extended discussion of the index.

[2] Thus, in case of the computation of the index for, say, German imports, we need, for the *unweighted average*, the percentages held by the exports to Germany in the total exports of the United States, Great Britain, etc. These percentages were taken throughout from the annual publication, *International Trade Statistics,* of the Economic Intelligence Service of the League of Nations. The "Summary Tables by Countries of Provenance and Destination" at the end of the volumes were found particularly useful in speeding up the work of writing down the percentages. For the computation of the *weighted average,* we need: (1) as denominator, the sum of the exports of the countries with which Germany trades, expressed in a common currency; this sum was calculated from the trade statistics in gold dollars published in the annual *Review of World Trade* by the Economic Intelligence Service of the League of Nations. And we need: (2) as numerator, the total imports of Germany from the United States, Great Britain, etc., expressed in the same common currency as the denominator. This figure was not taken from German statistics, but, for reasons of homogeneity, from the trade statistics of Germany's trading partners. The two previous steps in our calculations provided the necessary material for this seemingly cumbersome procedure. Thus, in order to obtain, for example, British exports to Germany expressed in gold dollars, we multiplied the percentage held by Germany in Great Britain's exports (as recorded previously for the computation of the unweighted average) by the gold dollar value of Great Britain's total exports (as recorded previously for the computation of the denominator of the weighted average) and divided by 100.

90 *National Power and Foreign Trade*

Economic Intelligence Service of the League of Nations[3] and is found by dividing the imports, as given by the German statistics (but converted into an international currency), by world imports.

The figure relevant for our analysis is obtained by dividing German imports, as given by the *export statistics of the other countries,*[4] through total world exports *minus German exports.* Whereas the figure generally calculated gives an answer to the question: How much of everything which is imported or exported is imported or exported by Germany?, the figure here computed answers the question: All countries except Germany being considered together, what is the proportion of their imports or exports accounted for by Germany?

This latter question seems to the writer to be as important as the first one, as it points out the importance of a certain country's trade for the rest of the world.[5]

The unweighted average is seen to have a meaning if we write expression (3) above in the following form:

$$U.A. = W.A. \cdot \frac{R}{100}$$

In this form we can consider the unweighted average as an expression of the importance of Germany's trade to the other countries, as shown by the weighted average corrected by the index of preference for small countries.

Indeed, if we consider that this importance depends not only upon the amount of trade conducted with other countries, but also upon the way in which this trade is distributed between large and small countries, the introduction of the index of preference as a corrective factor is fully justified. In this way the unweighted average may be looked at, not as an intermediate step in our calculations, but as its final outcome. It shows, so far as possible by purely quantitative methods, the aggregate "importance" of a country's trade to

---

[3] Cf., in particular, the annual publication, *Review of World Trade.*

[4] See above, n. 2, p. 89.

[5] Since the answer to the first question only is given by the available statistics, it is easily confused with the answer to the second question. The denominator of the fraction thus used is larger than it ought to be, and this leads to an underestimate of a country's importance to the rest of the world. The underestimate may be serious if the country holds an important place in world trade.

the economies of the other countries, the "importance" being conceived as the combined result of the amount of the country's trade and of its preference for small countries.

Before coming to the explanation of the figures, we have still to define clearly what we mean by a small or a large country. Our index is an index of preference for countries having a small foreign trade. This is actually what we would have had to measure if we had wanted to illustrate statistically the ideas expressed on and following page 29. If reliable statistics were available showing the levels of real incomes of the various states at different epochs, we could have calculated an index of preference of, say, German, English, etc., trade for countries with small real incomes, and in this way we could have tested our ideas with respect to the relationship of a power policy and the diversion of trade to *poor* countries. In the present unsatisfactory state of statistics of national real income, we employed at an earlier juncture a rough-and-ready method relying on Colin Clark's comparative study of national incomes.[6] As the states which are small with respect to territory and population but enjoy a high level of real income (for example, Belgium, Holland, Switzerland, Denmark, New Zealand, etc.) generally handle a considerable volume of foreign trade, however, an index of preference for the small trading nations turns out to be roughly representative for an index of preference for the countries which are *both small and poor*.

INTERPRETATION OF THE STATISTICS

The index has been computed for six great powers: the United States, the United Kingdom, Germany, France, Italy, and Japan, for the period from 1925 to 1938 and for 1913. The calculations are based on data for fifty-one countries which control from 90 to 95 per cent of world trade. In order to make the index more meaningful, no account was taken of the colonial or semicolonial countries, with the exception of India and the Southwest Pacific area. In 1938 Austrian trade, if reported separately, was added to German trade, leaving us for that year only fifty countries.

In the following we shall refer to the index of preference for small countries as simply "the index," to the unweighted average of the shares as the "average import or export share," and to the weighted

---

[6] See above, p. 37.

National Power and Foreign Trade

TABLE 1
INDICES OF PREFERENCE FOR SMALL OR LARGE TRADING COUNTRIES

		1913	1925	1926	1927	1928	1929	1930
Imports of:								
Germany	U.A.*	12.70	10.64	9.81	12.37	12.82	11.95	11.20
	W.A.†	16.12	8.46	7.55	10.22	9.78	9.28	8.39
	I.‡	**78.8**	**125.8**	**129.9**	**121.0**	**131.1**	**128.8**	**133.5**
England	U.A.	24.34	23.92	23.80	23.29	22.10	22.09	23.44
	W.A.	22.27	21.61	20.80	20.04	18.93	18.63	20.15
	I.	**109.3**	**110.7**	**114.4**	**116.2**	**116.7**	**118.4**	**116.3**
U. S. A.	U.A.	13.65	17.09	17.65	16.54	16.03	16.69	15.32
	W.A.	9.22	15.52	15.99	14.70	13.85	14.31	12.03
	I.	**148.1**	**110.1**	**110.4**	**112.5**	**115.7**	**116.6**	**127.3**
France	U.A.	6.70	4.73	4.77	4.39	4.73	4.97	5.31
	W.A.	6.68	5.09	5.16	4.73	5.07	5.43	6.19
	I.	**100.3**	**92.9**	**92.4**	**92.8**	**93.3**	**91.5**	**85.8**
Italy	U.A.	2.21	3.89	3.78	3.54	3.66	3.79	3.94
	W.A.	3.05	3.40	3.02	2.81	3.21	3.15	3.09
	I.	**72.5**	**114.4**	**125.2**	**126.0**	**114.0**	**120.3**	**127.5**
Japan	U.A.	1.33	1.85	1.98	1.79	1.78	1.84	1.70
	W.A.	1.83	3.31	3.43	3.05	3.11	2.82	2.49
	I.	**72.7**	**55.9**	**57.7**	**58.7**	**57.2**	**65.2**	**68.3**
Exports of:								
Germany	U.A.	17.02	12.83	13.63	13.58	14.54	14.98	15.34
	W.A.	16.89	8.14	9.40	9.35	10.48	10.71	12.14
	I.	**100.8**	**157.6**	**145.0**	**145.2**	**138.7**	**139.9**	**126.4**
England	U.A.	21.08	18.61	16.45	16.75	16.15	15.79	15.78
	W.A.	17.28	16.29	14.41	14.35	13.82	13.40	13.26
	I.	**122.0**	**114.2**	**114.2**	**116.7**	**116.9**	**117.8**	**119.0**
U. S. A.	U.A.	13.64	19.28	19.31	19.00	19.19	19.55	18.20
	W.A.	13.40	19.23	19.33	18.40	18.12	18.43	16.88
	I.	**101.8**	**100.3**	**100.0**	**103.3**	**105.9**	**106.1**	**107.8**
France	U.A.	5.14	4.51	5.02	5.05	4.92	4.60	4.60
	W.A.	5.72	4.89	4.82	5.31	5.25	4.94	4.91
	I.	**89.9**	**92.2**	**104.2**	**95.1**	**93.7**	**93.1**	**93.7**
Italy	U.A.	2.22	3.70	3.48	3.21	3.02	2.96	3.14
	W.A.	2.17	2.75	2.55	2.50	2.38	2.38	2.41
	I.	**102.3**	**134.5**	**136.5**	**128.4**	**126.9**	**124.4**	**130.3**
Japan	U.A.	1.27	1.98	1.97	2.02	1.86	2.02	2.16
	W.A.	1.56	2.99	3.14	2.92	2.85	2.87	2.75
	I.	**81.4**	**66.2**	**62.7**	**69.2**	**65.3**	**70.4**	**78.5**

* Unweighted average of percentage shares of imports from (exports to) Germany, England, etc., in total imports (exports) of fifty-one countries.
† Weighted average of percentage shares of imports from (exports to) Germany, England, etc., in total imports (exports) of fifty-one countries.
‡ Index of preference for large or small trading countries $\left(= \frac{\text{U.A.}}{\text{W.A.}} \cdot 100 \right)$.

1931	1932	1933	1934	1935	1936	1937	1938	
								Imports of:
9.83	9.95	10.07	11.47	11.48	11.89	11.92	14.94	Germany
7.81	7.96	8.00	8.65	8.31	7.43	7.53	9.87	
125.9	**125.0**	**133.8**	**134.7**	**138.2**	**160.0**	**158.3**	**151.4**	
25.48	25.41	26.23	25.57	24.87	25.25	23.92	24.67	England
22.18	21.41	21.99	21.87	22.07	22.65	20.06	21.13	
114.9	**118.7**	**119.3**	**116.9**	**112.7**	**111.5**	**119.2**	**116.8**	
14.73	13.74	13.70	13.63	14.84	15.56	15.61	13.79	U. S. A.
11.47	11.22	10.89	10.40	14.68	14.41	13.70	11.02	
128.4	**122.5**	**125.8**	**131.1**	**101.1**	**108.0**	**113.9**	**125.1**	
5.69	5.62	5.63	4.67	4.31	4.62	4.20	3.79	France
6.51	6.63	6.69	5.53	4.86	4.89	4.65	4.12	
87.4	**84.8**	**84.1**	**84.4**	**88.7**	**94.5**	**90.3**	**92.0**	
3.72	3.93	3.81	3.70	3.54	2.09	2.96	2.55	Italy
2.89	3.07	3.19	3.27	3.14	1.89	2.63	2.35	
128.7	**128.0**	**119.4**	**113.2**	**112.7**	**110.6**	**112.5**	**108.5**	
2.15	2.01	1.89	2.10	2.13	2.56	2.30	1.88	Japan
2.80	2.94	2.93	3.32	3.22	3.48	3.28	2.73	
78.8	**68.4**	**64.5**	**63.3**	**66.1**	**73.6**	**70.1**	**68.4**	
								Exports of:
16.00	15.05	14.18	13.03	14.25	16.56	15.80	17.70	Germany
13.60	12.04	11.46	10.09	9.82	10.04	9.66	10.88	
117.6	**125.0**	**123.7**	**129.1**	**145.1**	**164.9**	**163.6**	**162.7**	
15.13	16.47	17.85	17.80	17.69	16.31	15.45	15.41	England
12.25	13.04	13.88	14.21	14.52	14.19	13.10	13.29	
123.5	**126.3**	**128.6**	**125.3**	**121.8**	**114.9**	**117.9**	**116.0**	
16.82	15.85	14.92	15.88	16.00	16.27	17.04	18.35	U. S. A.
14.48	14.13	13.01	13.34	13.37	13.91	14.66	15.73	
116.2	**112.2**	**114.7**	**119.0**	**119.7**	**117.0**	**116.2**	**116.7**	
4.47	4.20	4.27	4.12	3.52	2.88	2.68	2.97	France
4.90	4.23	4.49	5.05	3.80	3.18	2.98	3.12	
91.2	**99.3**	**95.1**	**81.6**	**92.6**	**90.6**	**89.9**	**95.2**	
3.34	3.46	3.34	3.00	2.40	1.29	2.05	2.29	Italy
2.71	2.66	2.61	2.39	2.07	1.32	1.68	1.97	
123.6	**130.1**	**128.0**	**125.5**	**115.9**	**97.7**	**122.0**	**112.1**	
2.41	2.75	3.31	3.91	4.15	3.79	3.30	3.00	Japan
2.78	2.83	2.97	3.00	3.31	3.10	2.85	2.41	
86.7	**97.2**	**111.5**	**130.3**	**125.4**	**122.3**	**115.8**	**124.4**	

average of these shares as the "percentage in world trade," bearing in mind the difference between our third expression and the usual meaning of this term.[7]

The following main results appear from table 1:

1) In general a definite regularity appears to exist in the phenomenon the index intends to measure: In most of the series it is highly stable during the period 1925 to 1938, which otherwise has been marked by tremendous economic upheavals. The highest value of the index obtained is 164.9 for German exports in 1936. To find out one of the possibly lowest values, we have computed separately the index for Canada, the trade from which goes mainly to the two largest trading countries; for Canada we obtained a value of 37 for both imports and exports in the year 1937.

There is generally a rather close connection for any one country between the level and movements of the index for imports and for exports. One notable exception is Japan (see point 5).

So far as a preference for the small trading countries is concerned, we note that it prevails in the indices for all the big powers with the exception of France and, with respect to imports, with the exception of Japan. Any trade between a large and a small trading country leads to the power disequilibrium which we have described, since, whatever the volume of trade, it will always be more difficult for the small trading country to divert its trade than it will be for the large one. But we see now that the structure of the trade of most large countries is such as to emphasize this element of power already inhering in trade relations.

2) The most interesting single series is the German one. For both imports and exports, the index rises abruptly between 1913 and 1925. To a large extent this is to be explained by the fact that two of the main trading areas of Germany, i.e., eastern and southeastern Europe, were divided by the peace treaties of 1918 into a large number of small countries. Neither Britain nor the United States nor France had a large trade with these areas; consequently their indices were not greatly affected when they were broken up into small political units. Not unlike the German index, the Italian also rose substantially from 1913 to 1925. The index thus brings out with particular clarity the fact that the territorial stipulations of the peace treaties actually helped Germany and Italy—the vanquished and the so-called "frustrated victor"—to increase their potentialities of economic power.

The German indices reach their lowest value during the depression years, but it is noticeable that their general level is higher in and following 1925 than the indices of any other country, the Italian indices coming nearest to the German level. Thus, even before the conscious policy of increasing influence through a redistribution of foreign trade came into being, German commerce was structurally directed toward the small countries more than it was to large countries. In short, Germany found herself, in 1933, well situated to pursue a power policy through foreign trade.

From 1934 to 1936 the indices for German exports and for German imports both arrive by two abrupt jumps at record levels far beyond the indices of any other country. Imports lead in this process, but in time are outdistanced by the exports. This shows again that Germany initiated her trade drive by increasing imports from other countries, mainly those of southeastern Europe. Though the drive continued till 1938, the index, with some slight downward tendency, is more or less stable from 1936 on. This stability can be explained by Germany's expanding trade drive in the somewhat larger South American countries and by her increased buying for inventory from the United States during 1938.

Turning now to the average share in imports and exports, taken as an approximation to the aggregate "importance" of a country's trade to the economies of the other countries, we discover that the average German import share in other countries is larger in 1938, for the first time, than the American share, although the American percentage in world imports (the "weighted average") is far greater than the German one. A similar relationship holds for the German average share in exports with regard to the English share from 1936 to 1938 and to the American share in 1936. In both situations, the considerable inferiority of Germany with respect to the actual volume of her trade was more than compensated by the particular country-distribution she had succeeded in giving to her trade, so that the average share held in other countries was superior to that held by England and the United States.

The behavior of the German indices since the rise to power of National Socialism gives as good an instance as could be desired to illustrate the general principles of a power policy using foreign trade as its instrument.

3) The most stable series are the English and the French. The low level of the French indices is explained by the fact that the French colonies are not included in our calculations. The French series therefore have to be considered as pertaining to the volume and the country-distribution of noncolonial French trade; and it is interesting to note that this trade showed on the whole a preference for large trading countries. This is a consequence of the slight influence of French trade in the small trading countries of Europe and South America.

4) The Italian indices, as already noted, move in general on a high level, giving some support to the thesis that Italy was the only power which, because of the structure of its foreign trade, could have effectively opposed the German trade drive toward small European countries, especially those in southeastern Europe. One should not, however, over-rate the importance of the high level of the Italian indices; it is combined with a rather low percentage in world trade, so that the average share—

the indicator for the importance of Italy's trade with other countries—lies below all other countries, with the exception of Japanese imports.

A significant fact is that the fall of the Italian indices during the sanctions year, 1936, was slight for imports but considerable for exports. If all countries had reduced their trade with Italy to the same degree, the index would of course have shown no relevant variation. As it was, the United States and, above all, Germany did not participate in the sanctions, and hence Italian trade was directed more toward the larger trading countries than ordinarily. In 1938 the export index again goes down considerably, this time because of the annexation of Austria.

5) The striking fact about the Japanese indices is, first, their very low level until 1929. This shows that Japan was still trading mainly with the large trading countries, like the United States, and the relatively large Pacific trading countries, such as China, India, and Australia. After 1929 this remains true of the imports—some expansion toward the smaller Pacific countries is matched by a simultaneous expansion of imports from the United States—whereas the export index rises sharply and continuously, reaching a rather high level in 1934. Since then we observe a slight downward tendency. The rise of the index is thus intimately connected with the notorious trade drive of Japan during the depression. This drive involved imports as well as exports, but although it did not materially alter the country-distribution of Japanese imports, it did alter the exports distribution, which were directed much more than formerly toward the smaller Far Eastern countries (Thailand, Philippines, Netherlands Indies), toward Latin America (Cuba, Peru, Uruguay), and even toward small European countries (Finland, Austria, Norway).

When, for any country, the indices for imports and exports attain approximately the same level, this is not necessarily (though it probably is) an indication of the presence of bilateralism in the trade of this country, since, assuming a preference for small countries, this preference need not go to the same small countries for imports as for exports. When the levels of the indices diverge materially for imports and for exports, however, this is an almost certain indication of the absence of bilateralism. It can thus be seen that the expansion of Japanese trade was possible only through whatever triangularity remained in world trade. In particular, the payment for Japan's huge deficit in her trade with the United States, which provided her with important raw materials, semimanufactures, and industrial equipment, was rendered possible by her favorable balances with a great number of small countries all over the world.

Finally, our figures explain and justify the surprise generally felt in the early 'thirties, when experts, quoting the Japanese percentages of world trade, told the public that, after all, there had not been such a big expansion of Japanese trade. These percentages, indeed, rise from a low point in 1930 to a peak during the middle and late 'thirties (1937 for imports, 1935 for exports)—from 2.56 per cent (2.49 per cent) for imports and 2.67 per cent (2.75 per cent) for exports to only 3.88 (3.28) and 3.65 (3.31), respectively.[8] If we look, instead, at the unweighted average share of Japanese exports in the imports of other countries, we see that this figure has approximately doubled in the same interval, and beginning in 1935 was greater than both the French and Italian average shares. Thus, the moderate increase in the relative volume of Japanese exports did not tell the whole story; by directing the increase of her trade more toward smaller countries, Japan succeeded in increasing her influence in foreign countries more than would have corresponded to the relative increase in volume of her exports.

6) Whereas for Japan's exports there is a simultaneous increase of her share in world exports and of the index, for most of the other countries, and particularly for the three largest ones (United States, United Kingdom, and Germany), we find a negative correlation between the movement of the index and the percentage in world trade relating to one country's imports or exports. This is particularly evident for United States imports, for which the index shows important fluctuations almost exactly opposed to those of the percentage in world trade. As a result of these contrary movements, the unweighted average share is very stable. In particular, the drop in the American import index from 1934 to 1935 must be viewed in conjunction with the sudden and important revival of American imports in 1935. This will give a very rough indication: Of seventy-eight possible yearly variations for the import and export indices for Germany, the United Kingdom, and the United States from 1925 to 1938, it was found that fifty-seven (73 per cent) were in the direction opposite to the corresponding change of the percentage in world trade. Some more specific evidence in the same sense is that brought out by the fact that when the German export percentage reached its peak in 1931, the index reached its lowest point; the same holds for the imports of the United Kingdom in 1936, her exports in 1925, French imports in 1933, and approximately for the other series, with the exception of Italian exports and both Japanese series. The contention that an increase of the share of the largest trading countries in world trade was possible mainly through an increase of their trade amongst themselves thus seems to be well supported by statistical evidence. This accords with the *a priori* expectation of a greater elasticity on the part of the markets of the large countries.

---

[8] The figures in parentheses relate to our weighted average of the shares, the others are the usual percentages given by the League of Nations.

CHAPTER VI

Concentration upon Markets and Supply Sources of the Foreign Trade of Small or Weak Nations

In CHAPTER V we have seen the differing extents to which each of the large trading nations have directed their trade toward the smaller trading countries. By the same process we also covered the trends of the foreign trade of those countries which were likely to be the *subjects* of a policy using foreign trade as its instrument. Now we turn to the countries likely to have been the *objects* of such a policy. We shall try to examine what the particular position of these countries has been with respect to the attempt of one, or of a few, big trading nations to monopolize their trade.

METHOD OF MEASUREMENT

The concentration of a nation's trade depends on the number of countries with which it trades and on the more or less equal distribution of its trade among these countries. In other words, the phenomenon which we want to measure presents ideally the characteristics necessary for the application of our index of concentration, which is explained in Appendix A.

The imports (or exports) of a country from (or to) the other countries can be expressed as percentages of its total imports (or exports). The index is obtained by forming the sum of the squares of these percentages and by extracting the square root of this sum. It behaves in the following way: When a country's trade is completely monopolized by another country, the value of the index is $\sqrt{100^2} = 100$. The index would assume the value of zero if we had an infinite number of countries possessing each an infinitely small share in the trade of the country examined. If a nation trades with fifty countries, the smallest possible value of the index would be reached if all the fifty countries occupy the same percentage in the nation's trade, i.e., 2 per cent. The index would then be $\sqrt{50.2^2} = 14.14$. The upper limit of the index is, of course, again 100, which would be approached if forty-nine of the fifty states handle negligible amounts of trade with the nation considered, while one state has a virtual monopoly. Thus, when the number of countries increases, the upper limit of the index remains the same, while the lower limit decreases gradually. If the number of countries is constant, the index increases whenever a percentage x increases at the expense of some percentage smaller than x, i.e., whenever a relatively small percentage becomes still smaller and a relatively large percentage still larger.

To avoid misinterpretation, we must add one explanation. The index does *not* measure the strength of the monopoly position of the *largest exporting or importing country*. This monopoly position is the stronger:

1) the *greater* the percentage held by the monopolist country in the trade of a country X,

2) the *smaller* the concentration of the remaining part of X's trade, i.e., the less the monopoly country is confronted by other countries holding smaller but still important shares of the trade of country X.

An index of the strength of the monopolistic position of the largest exporting or importing country should thus: (1) vary directly with the percentage held by this country in the trade of X, and (2) vary *inversely* with the concentration of the remaining part of X's trade.

Our index satisfies the first of these conditions, but not the second. As an index of concentration of a country's trade, it varies directly with the concentration of the total trade and with the concentration of any part of this trade. It should therefore be considered as expressing the degree of *oligopoly, or oligopsony existing in a country's external market, monopoly being considered as a limiting case of oligopoly*.

From the construction of the index it will be clear that it is always higher than the percentage held by the largest importing or exporting country. It will be helpful to keep this in mind.

A further difficulty is connected with the definition of a "country" for the purposes of our index. If country X trades with Belgium and with the Belgian Congo, should the Congo be considered as a separate country, or should its percentage be added to the Belgian percentage? This question has a practical importance in our study mainly because the colonial territories of India and the Netherlands Indies often hold important percentages in the trade of the countries which we have examined. We have followed throughout the procedure of considering these territories as separate countries, since our index measures not only the political but also the geographical distribution of the trade of the various countries. Indeed, if only the political distribution had been considered, we should probably have lumped together in one country the whole British Empire, the countries of the Little Entente during the years in which it could be considered as a political unit, and Germany and Italy from 1936 on, etc. We have reversed the rule only when complete fusion or annexation took place. Thus, in the year 1938, Austria has been considered as being part of Germany.[1]

---

[1] Our source throughout has been the annual publication, *International Trade Statistics,* edited by the Economic Intelligence Service of the League of Nations. A purely statistical difficulty was presented by the ever-present percentage under the heading of "other countries." Fortunately, this item is important mainly in the large trading countries for which the index has not been calculated. For the countries which have been considered in our calculations, the item "other countries" is generally small and seldom exceeds 5 per cent of the total. The concentration would, of course, have been overstated if we had considered the item "other countries" as a single country. We have made the arbitrary assumption that it was constituted by a certain number of countries holding each 0.5 per cent of the imports or exports of the nation considered. Suppose, e.g., that the item "other countries" amounts to 5.2 per cent; then, we assume that it is composed of ten countries holding 0.5 per cent plus one country holding 0.2 per cent. Instead of $5.2^2 = 27.04$, we added, therefore, only $10 \times 0.5^2 + 0.2^2 = 2.54$ to the sum of the squares of the other percentages.

Our assumption probably still overstates the concentration, for, even among the percentages for individual countries, we often find figures smaller than 0.5 per cent of the exports or imports. But, by expanding the foregoing example, we see how small is the practical importance of the apparent difficulty. Let us suppose that the sum of the squares of the percentages relating to individual countries amounts to 900 (we choose purposely a rather low concentration); then the total sum of the squares is:

1) 927.04, if we consider the "other countries" as one single country,
2) 902.54, with our assumption, and
3) 900.00, when we consider all the percentages as infinitely small.

The indices of concentration are given by the square root of these figures and are, respectively:

1) 30.45   2) 30.04   3) 30.00

As the true index certainly lies nearer to the second than to the first figure and probably somewhere between the second and the third, we see that ordinarily the range of error is extremely small, especially if we disregard in our interpretation small movements of the index. When the item "other countries" exceeded 10 per cent, as, e.g., in Argentina's exports in 1913 and 1925, we have not calculated the index. (See also Appendix A.)

INTERPRETATION OF THE STATISTICS

The index has been calculated for a total of forty-four relatively small and weak countries for the years 1913, 1925, 1929, 1932, 1937, and 1938. We may remind the reader that 1932 is a particularly crucial year, as it is marked by the bottom of the great depression, by the Ottawa Agreements, and by the last struggles of the Weimar Republic.

To the results of our calculations, which are reproduced in table 2, we have also appended the index for Great Britain, the country the trade of which probably shows the widest spread and therefore gives an indication of the lower limit actually reached by our index. The average value for the English index for both imports and exports is 20. The highest value ascertained for the index is that for Irish exports, amounting to 97 in 1925 and never falling below 90. A wide range of variation is thus open to the index.

CONCENTRATION OF IMPORTS COMPARED TO THE CONCENTRATION OF EXPORTS

It will be noted that for every country the index is either stable or has a definite trend. Sudden jumps are very rare. The trends of the various national indices are, however, far from being uniform, and no definite general relationship could be established between the movements of the index and the business cycle.[2]

But one general feature can be pointed out: The concentration of exports has a tendency to be stronger—and often markedly stronger—than the concentration of imports. Of all the forty-four countries examined (we do not count the United Kingdom), only five—Lithuania, Switzerland, Rumania, Canada, and Nigeria—exhibit in general the opposite relationship. For the countries with a relatively low concentration, the level of the export and the import indices of concentration move at a roughly similar level. This is true for Norway, Sweden, Belgium, Netherlands, Czechoslovakia, Portugal, Austria, Hungary, Yugoslavia, Turkey, British Malaya, Netherlands Indies, and, recently, India. In addition, Peru, Ecuador, and Mexico, the foreign trade of which is strongly concentrated, were in the same position.

---

[2] See, however, below, p. 109.

TABLE 2

INDICES OF CONCENTRATION OF TRADE

		1913	1925	1929	1932	1937	1938
EUROPE—GROUP 1							
Bulgaria	I*	41.7	32.3	31.7	32.1	56.4	54.0
	E†	31.9	31.8	37.3	35.5	46.7	60.3
Hungary	I		38.9	35.2	34.0	35.8	44.5
	E		43.9	38.4	37.4	33.9	48.2
Rumania	I	48.6	33.5	34.1	35.1	37.3	42.1
	E	36.7	28.4	34.8	29.1	27.6	33.2
Yugoslavia	I	54.6‡	35.4	33.3	32.5	38.4	43.6
	E	50.0‡	37.7	35.6	37.4	32.0	45.5
Greece	I	36.9	29.8	27.4	28.3	34.1	36.5
	E	34.3	39.5	37.1	36.2	38.1	45.3
Turkey	I		31.2	29.1	33.2	46.3	50.6
	E		37.3	33.5	29.6	41.3	47.6
EUROPE—GROUP 2							
Netherlands	I	37.8	34.9	36.6	36.2	29.8	30.3
	E	54.1	39.5	34.9	34.6	31.7	32.2
Belgium	I	31.1	32.2	31.8	31.3	25.6	27.1
	E	37.3	31.8	30.0	31.2	28.8	28.8
Austria	I		31.7	32.7	31.1	26.7	
	E		27.9	27.8	27.9	27.2	
Czechoslovakia	I		35.8	32.2	31.6	23.4	26.0
	E		32.5	29.2	26.3	23.7	26.6
Switzerland	I	40.8	32.1	34.7	35.2	30.3	32.8
	E	33.4	31.6	27.9	26.5	26.6	26.9
Poland	I		37.4	34.2	28.7	25.5	30.3
	E		44.9	37.2	29.1	28.7	33.2

* Imports.   † Exports.   ‡ 1912 figures.

TABLE 2—(*Continued*)

		1913	1925	1929	1932	1937	1938
EUROPE—GROUP 3							
Norway	I	43.8	35.8	36.6	34.3	34.6	34.5
	E	33.8	35.1	33.6	32.7	35.6	35.9
Sweden	I	44.2	38.2	39.7	37.2	32.3	35.7
	E	39.6	35.1	33.5	32.3	33.2	33.9
Denmark	I	44.1	36.8	39.9	36.8	46.2	44.1
	E	62.4	59.9	60.4	65.9	56.7	59.4
Estonia	I		40.8	36.7	38.0	34.3	38.5
	E		43.2	47.7	46.4	46.7	47.4
Latvia	I		45.6	44.7	40.9	36.8	44.8
	E		45.3	42.4	44.1	53.2	55.0
Lithuania	I		57.0	62.8	57.3	50.5	48.9
	E		58.4	51.2	44.0	38.3	41.5
Finland	I	51.9	40.8	43.9	37.6	34.6	34.9
	E	42.9	42.7	43.4	49.6	48.9	48.9
OTHER EUROPEAN COUNTRIES							
Portugal	I	36.3	37.2	37.2	33.7	30.9	30.6
	E	36.9	35.9	33.4	33.4	31.7	31.3
Spain	I	31.1	30.0	28.4	25.7		
	E	34.8	32.7	34.1	35.2		
Albania	I		78.0	49.7	43.6	32.6	41.2
	E		65.1	65.6	67.8	79.6	70.2
United Kingdom	I	27.7	25.4	23.6	21.5	21.0	21.8
	E	22.0	20.5	20.2	19.1	19.5	19.6

TABLE 2—(*Continued*)

		1913	1925	1929	1932	1937	1938
				BRITISH EMPIRE			
Eire...............	I		81.3	78.7	77.0	51.5	52.5
	E		97.2	92.2	96.3	90.9	92.7
Canada.............	I	67.6	68.3	70.5	62.0	63.5	65.3
	E	62.7	53.2	51.1	51.4	56.1	53.5
Ceylon.............	I	52.2	42.0	36.6	36.7	36.6	35.5
	E	50.0	50.1	45.7	51.9	49.4	55.4
India...............	I	65.2	54.2	45.5	41.6	38.6	38.5
	E	31.4	32.0	30.4	32.9	37.9	37.8
British Malaya.......	I	33.8	45.0	38.4	42.0	40.2	38.3
	E	38.3	53.2	46.5	33.5	47.5	37.0
Australia............	I	54.7	51.1	47.7	44.9	46.6	46.2
	E	48.2	46.9	41.4	55.3	51.7	56.3
New Zealand.........	I	62.1	56.3	53.7	54.8	54.0	52.8
	E	79.7	80.4	74.5	88.0	76.6	84.0
Egypt..............	I	36.1	31.5	28.8	30.1	29.1	29.9
	E	47.2	48.5	40.4	42.2	36.3	38.1
Nigeria.............	I	70.2	74.8	71.2	74.8	65.3	67.1
	E	66.0	60.6	51.9	46.1	50.5	68.3
Union of South Africa.	I	58.6	52.9	47.8	49.2	47.9	47.8
	E	88.8	58.7	66.7	82.5	79.4	75.9

TABLE 2—(*Concluded*)

		1913	1925	1929	1932	1937	1938
		SOUTH AMERICA§					
Argentina¶..........	I	40.7	36.8	36.2	31.5	31.3	30.6
	E			40.2	42.5	36.6	37.6
Bolivia..............	I	45.1	38.9	42.3	37.5	38.3	37.3
	E	81.5	81.2	78.6	83.0	64.9	66.5
Brazil..............	I	37.1	38.9	40.3	38.7	38.7	39.0
	E	40.9	49.0	46.2	49.0	42.6	41.8
Chile‖..............	I	43.4	38.7	41.3	34.2	41.8	40.6
	E	49.5	53.2	32.0	44.2		
Colombia...........	I	42.1	55.3	51.0	49.4	53.9	55.8
	E	59.0	82.9	75.8	76.4	59.9	61.5
Ecuador.............	I	47.6	51.6	47.8	60.4	48.0	44.3
	E	46.6	45.9	49.0	48.5	42.9	44.0
Peru...............	I	43.9	45.4	50.6	37.1	43.1	42.2
	E	52.4	50.9	41.6	43.1	37.3	37.7
Uruguay.............	I	36.9	37.7	38.7	32.6	31.6	29.1
	E	35.8	37.0	36.1	38.6	35.1	38.3
		OTHER COUNTRIES					
Cuba...............	I	56.2	63.8	60.0	56.0	69.1	71.3
	E	80.8	77.7	76.3	73.1	81.5	77.3
Mexico.............	I	55.0	71.3	70.1	65.6	64.6	61.1
	E	78.2	76.4	62.7	66.5	58.4	68.7
Netherlands Indies....	I	42.1	32.8	32.8	34.2	36.4	34.1
	E	38.1	37.2	33.3	32.7	35.7	32.4
Philippines..........	I	52.5	59.7	64.6	66.0	60.6	69.4
	E	43.0	73.9	76.3	87.1	82.2	78.0

§ The index could not be calculated for Paraguay and Venezuela because of the important transit trade of these countries, handled by Argentina and Aruba, respectively. The ultimate destination or origin of this trade is not given.
¶ The data for 1913 and 1925 are not sufficiently detailed to warrant the computation of the index.
‖ The index has not been computed for the exports of 1937 and 1938 because of the important item guano, which is left undetailed with respect to countries.

Finally, we have counted twenty-three countries for which the export-concentration is usually or often markedly higher than the import-concentration.[3] Most of these are countries with highly concentrated trade. To bring this out more clearly, let us take all the countries the concentration of which, either for exports or imports, is usually above 40. We find twenty such countries,[4] of which fifteen show a greater spread for imports than for exports. Our statistics therefore warrant the conclusion that, for small countries with a relatively high foreign trade concentration, imports have a greater tendency to spread over various countries than exports.

This gives a cue concerning the connection between the concentration of trade upon countries and upon commodities. Although the latter type of concentration has definite meaning, it is awkward to deal with it statistically because of the difficulty of defining a commodity or a product. But we know that the greater part of the exports of countries with which we are concerned consists mainly of a few staple products upon which these countries have specialized, whereas their imports include a wide variety of finished products, raw materials, and foodstuffs. Therefore, the concentration of their exports according to commodities is higher than that of their imports. Since we find that the same relationship prevails for the concentration according to countries, we reach the conclusion that there is a positive correlation between the concentration of foreign trade according to countries and the concentration of foreign trade according to commodities.

This relationship holds with respect to exports only. We find, indeed, that all the countries having a varied commodity-composition of their export *as well as* of their import trade show also a low export-concentration with respect to countries.

The conclusion which we reach conflicts with what might at first sight be considered a plausible view: that specialization of a country's production for exports upon one or a very few commodities would permit this country to supply the whole world with these

[3] Finland, Estonia, Latvia, Denmark, Eire, Poland, Albania, Bulgaria, Spain, Greece, Ceylon, Australia, New Zealand, Egypt, South Africa, Philippines, Argentina, Bolivia, Brazil, Colombia, Cuba, Chile, Uruguay.

[4] Albania, Finland, Estonia, Latvia, Lithuania, Denmark, Eire, Bolivia, Brazil, Colombia, Ecuador, Cuba, Mexico, Canada, Ceylon, Australia, New Zealand, Nigeria, South Africa, Philippines.

commodities. On the other hand, it would seem natural that if a country trades mostly with another single country it would have a comparative advantage in a large number of products and would therefore have rather diversified exports. It would follow, then, that a dependence of exports upon one product would be tempered by a large geographical spread of exports, whereas a dependence of exports upon one country would be somewhat compensated by a diversified structure of the commodity-composition of exports.

In the actual world we see that the contrary happens: The correlation between the country-concentration and the commodity-concentration of foreign trade is positive instead of negative. In proceeding to an explanation of this, which we need not seek far to find, let us note that the foregoing reasoning is built on unrealistic assumptions since it overlooks the enormous differences in industrialization and in size of the various countries.

Although, as we shall see later, a considerable proportion of world trade can be considered as an exchange of foodstuffs and raw materials against foodstuffs and raw materials, there is generally but little direct exchange between countries the productive structure of which is mainly built upon the genetic and extractive industries.[5] As, in addition, the number of agricultural countries is very large, a nation takes up with every step in its industrialization a wide range of new trade connections without losing its old ones, since it may continue to send abroad substantial amounts of raw materials and foodstuffs and build part of its trade upon the exchange of manufactures against manufactures. But since the exports of an industrialized country are always more diversified than those of an agricultural or raw-material-producing country, the connection of low country-concentration and low commodity-concentration for the exports of industrial countries is easily explained.

But, if a small country specializes in a few staples, its produce might be insufficient to satisfy the entire demand of even a single large country, whereas the varied demand of the small country might best be filled by supplies from a large number of countries. These considerations bring out once more the importance of taking account more frequently, in the reasoning about international trade, of the factor of difference in size of the various countries.

---

[5] See below, pp. 126 ff.

We see here that the complementarity between two economies is very often, at least for the exports of one of the two countries, of the type which we have termed exclusive.[e] In other words, we do not have a complementarity between broad types of economies, the one agricultural and the other manufacturing, so that a given agricultural country can be considered as complementary to *any one* of the manufacturing countries. World trade is built, rather, in large proportion upon the reliance of the export products of one particular country upon the prosperity and tastes of one other individual country. New Zealand butter, Philippine sugar, and Bulgarian tobacco were not, in general, marketed in "industrial countries," but they were very specifically marketed in England, the United States, and Germany, respectively; possibilities of diversion from one of these countries to another hardly existed to any relevant extent.

These findings lead to an important conclusion: The existing pattern of world trade tends to correlate dependence upon a few countries which in turn depend upon a few products; it also brings about conditions in which the availability of alternative markets is seriously impaired. Under the condition of unchecked national sovereignties, this pattern therefore provides large opportunities for the exercise of economic pressures.

The tendency of exports of the smaller countries to be more concentrated than their imports is certainly in part natural. It could hardly be considered as an effect of conscious policy on the part of such countries as Australia or New Zealand. In many instances, however, it might be the outcome of a policy which, trying to spread trade more evenly over the various countries, was, because of the underlying natural tendency, more successful in importing than in exporting. In this category the figures for Eire are especially revealing. It can be assumed that the Irish government endeavored to disentangle the economy of the country from its extreme dependence upon Great Britain. In 1925, the year following the Irish independence, we find both the Irish indices at extremely high levels (although already the export index was at 97.2—higher than the import index, which stood at 81.3). In 1938 the import index had fallen to 52.2, whereas the export index had decreased only a few points, to 92.7. The attempts of South American nations to diversify

---

[e] See above, p. 31.

the commodity-structure of their exports for reasons of economic security are well known. The same motive may well induce a country to spread its trade among many countries, since the movements of the business cycle and changes in demand are not likely to coincide exactly in all countries. In addition, the desire to avoid political dependence on one country pushes policy in the same direction. Because of the "exclusive complementarity" which we have noted, however, this policy was not very successful so far as exports are concerned. This failure, together with the relative success of the policy with respect to imports, lends support to our contention that bilateralism is an important means of developing a power policy. *Indeed, if county A holds an important share in country B's exports, it can rely to a large degree upon the inability of B to divert its exports to third countries.* By the device of *bilateralism,* a country may then artificially secure or maintain a similarly dominating position in the *imports* of B, a position which would have been difficult if not impossible to obtain or to retain by normal trading methods.

ANALYSIS ACCORDING TO GROUPS OF COUNTRIES

We shall now examine in more detail the indices of concentration of various countries, dividing our inquiry into three headings: Europe, British Empire, and South America.

Europe.—We have calculated the indices for all the smaller European states, i.e., for all European countries except Great Britain, Germany, U. S. S. R., France, and Italy. The indices for Portugal, Spain, and Albania have been computed for the sake of completeness, but they will not be commented upon here. Eire is counted with British Empire countries. This gives a total of nineteen countries (eighteen in 1938 because of the Anschluss). Since every country yields two indices, one for imports and one for exports, we have in all, thirty-eight indices (thirty-six in 1938) the movements of which, from year to year, can be analyzed as in the table on the next page.

Thus, from 1925 to 1932, the smaller European countries show on the whole a tendency to lessen the concentration of their trade. There is not a single country showing an increase of both its import and export concentration either from 1925 to 1929 or from 1929 to 1932. This indicates that the range of markets was widening for European countries, the trade of which was generally compressed within narrow regional limits after World War I. For certain countries, this movement continued after 1932, but, for another group, it is reversed. Compared with 1932, this group is still a minority in 1937, but becomes a majority in 1938 owing to what was practically an all-round increase in the index from 1937 to 1938.

The detailed examination of the movement of the indices for the individual countries is facilitated if we distinguish three groups

CHANGES IN TRADE CONCENTRATION INDICES OF EUROPEAN COUNTRIES

	Number of countries showing decrease	Number of countries showing increase	Number of countries showing no significant change*	Total
1925–1929	21	8	9	38
1929–1932	20	6	12	38
1932–1937	19	12	7	38
1932–1938	12	19	5	36
1937–1938	3	24	9	36

* Change of less than unity.

of countries the trade of which is distributed according to three distinct patterns. The first consists of those countries in which the position of Germany has always been or has become dominant to the point that no other nations hold anything approaching a substantial share in the imports or exports of these countries. To this category belong all the countries of southeastern Europe with the exception of Albania. Secondly, we have a group of nations the trade of which is rather evenly spread over a number of countries. This includes the five small industrial countries, Belgium, Netherlands, Switzerland, Austria, Czechoslovakia, and also Poland. Thirdly, there is a group in which practically an Anglo-German duopoly prevailed, the shares of German and English trade taken together exceeding 50 per cent of the total trade. This group is made up of the Baltic and Scandinavian countries. The fundamental result of our figures shows that from 1925 to 1938 the concentration of trade has increased substantially for the first group of countries, has decreased for the second group, has had no definite trend for the third.

If we compare the movements of the various national indices from 1929 to 1938, the most striking difference is seen to be between the first and the second group of countries. The steep increases of the indices for the southeastern European countries reflect, of course, the increase of the German percentage in their trade and, as such, tell us nothing new. But by its generality the index permits an instructive comparison with the developments which took place simultaneously in other countries.

The indices of the second group show an all-round decline, which is still more evident when we compare the figures for 1937 with the "pre-Hitler" indices. In 1938, indeed, the annexation of Austria and the ensuing combination of the German and Austrian trade percentages make for a uniform increase in the indices, which is rather marked in Czechoslovakia and Poland.[7] The Czechoslovakian indices for 1937 are the lowest which we have found for any of the countries which might be considered as the "objects" of a power policy. Their level even approaches that of the British indices. Since Germany also holds the biggest percentage in the trade of the countries of the second group, the fall of the indices means generally that the reduction in Germany's share was made possible by an increase in the percentages of many other countries concurrently.

The difference in the behavior of the concentration indices for the first and second groups of countries can be ascribed to three factors. In the first place, the southeastern European countries had no common frontier with Germany until 1938, and may therefore not have held a particularly grave view of the effect of German commercial penetration. But the countries in the second group were all immediate neighbors of Germany and, as such, were the first potential victims of German aggression. It is also in this group that we find the only small European countries, with the exception of Sweden, which, in an effort to increase their overseas trade, have negotiated and signed agreements with the United States under the Reciprocal Trade Agreements Program.[8] Evidence, however, also exists that the countries in the first group, after having welcomed at first the massive German purchases of their agricultural surplus

---

[7] The annexation of Austria is also in great part responsible for the sudden increase in the Hungarian index from 1937 to 1938, whereas for the Balkan countries it simply adds impetus to a trend already manifest in the former years.

[8] The following are the countries and the dates on which they signed the agreements: Belgium, February 27, 1935; Netherlands (agreements comprising also the Dutch colonial territories), December 20, 1935; Switzerland, December 20, 1935; Czechoslovakia, March 7, 1938. Cf. Margaret S. Gordon, *Barriers to World Trade* (New York, 1941), p. 395.

products, soon realized the dangers of an exclusive German domination of their trade. They tried repeatedly to reverse the trend to which their foreign trade and thereby their entire economic structure was subjected, mainly by devaluing their currencies in the transactions with the free countries and by granting to exporters the privilege of retaining a certain proportion of the "devisen" obtained. But these policies were largely unsuccessful.[9]

This brings us to the second factor. The countries of the second group, although concerned over the dangers of too great a concentration of their trade upon Germany, were economically better prepared to resist it. Their economies were industrialized and their exports able to compete with similar exports from other regions of the world. Although the level of the concentration of their trade was not generally lower in 1929 than that of the southeastern European countries, the range of their trade connections in western Europe and in overseas countries was much wider. Finally, here again the fact that their exports were more varied has helped the countries of the second group to spread their exports more evenly over their various trading partners.

Until now our explanation has taken into account only the intentions of the various small countries and their capacity to carry out their intentions. When, however, we try to show why certain animals are the victims of the wolf, it is not sufficient to analyze the willingness and the capacity of the various possible victims to escape from the wolf, but it is necessary to investigate the varying appetite of the wolf with regard to his prospective victims. Here, again, the available evidence favors the countries of the second group. Their economies, indeed, did not present that type of complementarity to the German economy which was considered essential by Nazi economists for the building up of "sound" trade relations. Their exports to Germany consisted to a considerable degree of manufactured articles, an item which Germany endeavored to eliminate as far as possible.[10] These factors and the close economic contact of the countries in question with the Western world did not make them very suitable objects for the German methods of economic penetration.

[9] Cf. Royal Institute of International Affairs, *South Eastern Europe* (London, 1940), pp. 116–118.

[10] See below, pp. 137–138.

The situation is somewhat different with the Baltic and Scandinavian countries, which form our third European group. Their economies, being rich in agricultural and raw material resources, met the essential conditions for German penetration. Politically, also, they were considered as lying in the "German space." The trend of the concentration index of these countries is not a definite one. Little variation exists for Norway, Sweden, Finland, and Estonia. The marked increases of the indices for Latvian exports and Danish imports are due to a strong rise in the English percentages. Finally, we notice a marked decrease in the Lithuanian index because of a heavy decline in the German share, which was not entirely compensated by the concomitant rise of the British share. Thus, the picture presented by our figures shows the lack of success of German economic penetration in this group of countries. The presence of Great Britain as a big alternative market in their external trade provided for them the defensive weapon which was entirely absent in the Balkans.

Of course, an active policy of opposition to the German trade drive on the part of Great Britain and France would have changed matters in the Balkans and would have relieved the precarious economic situation of Lithuania, which, because of its energetic handling of the Nazi agitators in Memel, went through a period of German blockade from 1933 to 1936. But how far such a policy was removed from the intentions of British policy at that epoch may be seen from the following passage of an authoritative report on the Baltic states: "The principal feature of interest during these years (1930–1937) was the struggle between Germany and the United Kingdom for markets in this area. In this the United Kingdom was helped by the fact that sterling was, and the Reichsmark was not, a convertible currency. It consequently became vitally important, from a monetary point of view, that the Baltic States should increase their exports to the United Kingdom by every means in their power, or at any rate prevent them . . . falling off. . . . This increased the bargaining power of the United Kingdom when the time came to negotiate commercial agreements with these countries."[11]

This quotation is particularly revealing in its characterization of British policy in the countries selected as objects for German eco-

---

[11] Royal Institute of International Affairs, *The Baltic States* (London, 1938), p. 164.

nomic penetration. It intimates that Great Britain not only failed to assist these countries in their desire to counter the German drive by submitting offers to them at least as attractive as the German ones, but that Great Britain actually drove a bargain out of the desire of these countries to trade with her, a desire which she considered merely as a "monetary" phenomenon. It is indeed surprising, and explicable only by the desperate attempts of the smaller European countries to escape German commercial domination, that with this shortsighted policy Great Britain did not lose more ground to Germany than she actually did.

British Empire.—Under this heading we consider ten countries: Canada, Ceylon, India, British Malaya, Australia, New Zealand, Union of South Africa, Egypt, Nigeria, and Eire.

For all these countries, with the exception of British Malaya, Great Britain is the most important export market. For Canada, the British and American percentages are about equal, the American share having a tendency to be slightly higher. With respect to imports, Great Britain ranks second to the United States in Canada, to India in Ceylon, and to the Dutch East Indies in Malaya.

The most interesting feature of the concentration indices for the countries of the British Empire is the divergence in behavior of the import and export indices. When we compare 1937 with 1913 we find that the export indices maintain, on the whole, their rather high level, whereas the import indices all show more or less important decreases. This result is brought about in two periods: from 1913 to 1929 and from 1929 to 1938. With one exception, that of British Malaya, which increases its orientation toward the United States, the 1913 to 1929 period shows a general decrease in both the import and export indices. From 1929 to 1938 most of the import indices are stationary, whereas the export indices rise substantially for all countries, with the exception of Malaya and Egypt. It is noteworthy that the upward trend of the export indices is most in evidence from 1929 to 1932, i.e., before the Ottawa Agreement could make itself felt. Actually, it seems that the economic and monetary development of the depression was responsible for the reversal of the downward trend and that, with the exception of Nigeria, the Ottawa Agreement did not exercise an appreciable influence upon the concentration of the foreign trade in British colonies and dominions.

This means that it was the depression with its new trade barriers which foiled the previously noticeable tendency to develop new markets for the countries of the British Empire. It may also be interesting to note that in comparison with 1913 the relative positions of the import and export indices have been changed in a number of countries: for Canada, Ceylon, India, Australia, and Nigeria, the import index exceeded the export index in 1913, whereas the opposite relationship prevailed by 1938.[12] This illustrates further our previous remarks about the difficulty of shifting exports and the tendency of imports to spread out more evenly over a number of countries.

South America.—The period from 1913 to 1925 is the only one during which an upward movement of the indices seems to have been prevalent. This is an obvious reflection of the increase of the United States' position in the foreign trade of the countries under consideration. In all the following periods a somewhat irregular tendency toward a decrease predominates. From 1925 to 1929 it is slight, though visible, for the export indices and reflects the widening of the markets for the various South American countries during the prosperity period. Exactly the opposite movement occurs from 1929 to 1932, when the depression forced the reduced exports of these countries back to their traditional customers. A similar movement was noted previously for the countries of the British Empire. But, from 1929 to 1932 we observe a decrease in most of the import indices, which is traceable to the sharp decline of the usually dominating share of the United States. Exports from the United States to these countries, being generally goods with a high income elasticity, were the first to suffer from the curtailment of the purchasing power of these countries. In the revival, which came after 1932, the United States regained only partly the position it had lost in 1929, trade drives by Germany and Japan in the meantime having gained this trade.[13] This latter development must be seen against the background of traditional Anglo-American domination of the external trade of Latin America. England and the United States together

---

[12] For Malaya the inverse development took place, but the 1938 import index is clearly exceptionally low because of the reduction of the American share due to the 1938 recession.

[13] In addition, the regional trade between the South American countries has increased somewhat in numerous instances.

account for 40 to 80 per cent of the exports and imports of the countries during the years under consideration, the United States generally holding the first place, except in Argentina and Uruguay. Under these circumstances the German and Japanese advances during the 'thirties necessarily led to a decrease of the concentration of the foreign trade of these countries.[14]

Indeed, in one important respect the parallel between Germany's trading policy in the Balkans and that in South America does not hold. Although it is true that, except for technicalities, her trading methods and their economic basis and success have been the same in the two areas, in the Balkans Germany's aim was complete economic domination, whereas in the Latin American countries it could be only the undermining of the traditional Anglo-American domination. This, in conjunction with the geographical factor, may also explain why the latter countries resorted much less to defensive measures such as those employed—unsuccessfully—by the Balkan countries against German penetration.[15] The difference in the situation is well brought out by the increase of the concentration indices in the Balkan countries and their simultaneous decrease in the majority of the Latin American countries subject to German penetration.

In computing our index of concentration, we wished to bring out, for purposes of comparison, one single feature in the structure of the foreign trade of the various small countries which were patently the objects of a policy of commercial domination on the part of the big trading nations. Beyond the relationship between concentration of exports and concentration of imports upon which we have commented, our investigation has not permitted us to find a great number of common trends. Only from 1925 to 1929 can we speak of a general tendency pointing toward a decrease of the foreign trade concentration of the various countries. Subsequently, the trade of the countries of southeastern Europe only shows a sharply rising concentration. With this important exception the formation of commercial empires, which has often been considered as a characteristic of the 'thirties, has not materially affected the concentration of the foreign trade of the other small countries which we have examined.

---

[14] This decrease is particularly evident if we compare the figures of 1938 with those of 1929, a decrease of the *import* indices, a result of cyclical phenomena, having, in 1929, already taken place.

[15] See above, p. 112.

CHAPTER VII

The Commodity Structure of World Trade

In the two preceding chapters we have tried to analyze statistically certain features of the geographical distribution of world trade. We shall now turn our attention to the statistical analysis of a question concerning the commodity structure of world trade which has great political as well as economic importance.

According to a traditional conception, world trade is based essentially upon the division of labor between industrial and agricultural countries, or, differently expressed, upon the exchange of manufactures against foodstuffs and raw materials. This characterization of world trade has often been disputed on the ground that much of the trade of the industrial countries goes to other industrial countries and that world trade consists, therefore, to a large extent, in an exchange of manufactures against manufactures. Although both these opinions are simple assertions of facts with an essentially quantitative content, they have not yet had thorough statistical testing.

In the following we first present the nature of our test. We then give the main result brought out by our calculations for world trade as a whole. These figures are then broken up into the statistics for groups of countries and for several single important countries. The special historical interest centering around British foreign trade, together with the easy availability of adequate statistical material, induces us, in addition, to apply our method to English foreign trade statistics from the middle of the nineteenth century onward.

In a final section we try to bring out the rather mischievous role played in recent history by the traditional conception of the structure of world trade, especially with respect to German economic policy.

Method of Measurement

The statement that world trade consists mainly of an exchange of manufactures against foodstuffs and raw materials is somewhat ambiguous. A more precise formulation of its actual meaning can be

118 *National Power and Foreign Trade*

given in the following terms: Most countries, according to their "agricultural" or "industrial" character, *either* export foodstuffs and raw materials against imports of manufactures *or* import foodstuffs and raw materials against exports of manufactures. When, in the following, we speak of the share of the exchange of manufactures against foodstuffs and raw materials (which we shall call also the "traditional type of exchange") in total world trade, this should be interpreted as the degree to which the traditional view of the structure of world trade is found to be true.

The measurement of the extent to which world trade is based on the "traditional type of exchange" can proceed along lines made familiar by the measurement of bilateralism used by the Economic Intelligence Service of the League of Nations.[1]

The method consists in dividing the trade of each country into three categories:

1) total import or export balance;
2) imports and exports which offset one another in trade with individual countries;
3) balances in trade with individual countries not reflected by the aggregate balance (category 1), i.e., balances with opposite sign, offsetting one another.

The second category comprises the trade which balances bilaterally; the third, the trade which balances triangularly, whereas the first category contains the trade in commodities which does not balance at all against other commodities, but which is balanced—bilaterally or triangularly—against other items in the balance of payments.

If one calculates the three categories for all countries, he finds by addition the proportions in total world trade of trade balancing bilaterally, trade balancing triangularly, and trade balanced by the so-called "invisible items" of the balance of payments.

A similar method can be applied to the problem before us. The import and export trade of every country may be subdivided by commodity groups instead of by countries. In particular, the *International Classification of Brussels,* established in 1913, provides such

---

[1] Cf. *Review of World Trade*, 1932–1936 (annual volumes); cf. also Folke Hilgerdt, "The Approach to Bilateralism—A Change in the Structure of World Trade," *Index,* Vol. X (1935), pp. 175–188.

a subdivision in broad classes of merchandise: (1) live animals, (2) foodstuffs, (3) materials, raw and partly manufactured, (4) manufactured articles, (5) precious metals. By considering merchandise only (i.e., by excluding the fifth class), and by lumping together classes (1), (2), and (3) in the import and export statistics of each country, we obtain a broad dichotomy of foodstuffs and raw materials (products of primary industry), on the one hand, and manufactures (products of secondary industry), on the other.

If we now extend the concept of bilateralism to the two commodity groups under consideration, we have again a division of total trade in three categories:

1) the trade balance, positive or negative, i.e., that amount of trade which does not consist of exchange of commodities against commodities but of commodities against "invisible items."

2) the compensated commodity trade which might be called "bilateral with respect to commodity groups." It falls into two classes:

    a) the exchange of foodstuffs and raw materials against foodstuffs and raw materials,

    b) the exchange of manufactured products against manufactured products.

3) the compensated commodity trade which by analogy might be called triangular with respect to commodity groups. It comprises that part of trade which is not offset by "bilateral balancing" *within* the two commodity groups (a and b of class 2) but which is balanced *between* them. This part represents precisely the "traditional type" of exchange of manufactured products against foodstuffs and raw materials.[2]

---

[2] This includes the exchange between manufactured industrial products and manufactured foodstuffs, the latter being included in class (2) of the Brussels classification. The importance of manufactured foodstuffs has probably greatly increased in recent years, although, in the absence of sufficient statistical material, it is difficult to estimate the magnitude of this increase. Of the larger countries, only the United States lists manufactured foodstuffs as a separate commodity group. But the introduction of industrial methods into agriculture, or of new stages of transformation of crude agricultural products, only differentiates the agricultural character of a country; it does not impair it. If flour instead of grain is shipped in exchange for industrial machinery, this does not affect materially the traditional pattern of the international division of labor. In testing the extent to which this type of division of labor still predominates, it is necessary to classify manufactured foodstuffs with foodstuffs and not with manufactures. The inclusion of the partly manufactured materials with raw materials by the Brussels classification is from our point of view also warranted. The partly manufactured articles include, indeed, mainly crude metals (instead of minerals), scrap materials, and crude chemical materials, such as potash, ammonia, etc.

The drawing of a dividing line between manufactures and industrial materials involves, of course, a certain amount of arbitrariness, but, as will be seen, this degree of arbitrariness is certainly less than that implied in the only other method available for the measurement of our phenomenon.

To make our procedure clearer, let us give a few schematic illustrations. If we supposed, first, the existence of a trade balance in equilibrium and took the limiting case in which trade consisted of nothing but an exchange of foodstuffs and raw materials against manufactured products, then, the trade statistics of the country would result in the following picture:

SCHEME I

	Imports	Exports
Foodstuffs and raw materials.....................	100	0
Manufactured products	0	100
	100	100

But the "traditional type of exchange" would be eliminated if the two commodity groups balanced independently, as, e.g., in the following example:

SCHEME II

	Imports	Exports
Foodstuffs and raw materials....................	20	20
Manufactured products	80	80
	100	100

In the normal case we obtain the exchange of manufactures against manufactures by doubling the smaller item of the two opposite figures relating to imports and exports of manufactures. The exchange of foodstuffs and raw materials against foodstuffs and raw materials is obtained in a similar way, and the traditional type of exchange is found by balance. Thus, let us assume that the trade statistics present the following picture:

SCHEME III

	Imports	Exports
Foodstuffs and raw materials....................	80	30
Manufactured products	20	70
	100	100

The total trade of 200 can then by subdivided as follows:

Exchange of foodstuffs and raw materials against foodstuffs and raw materials...	60
Exchange of manufactures against manufactures.................	40
Exchange of manufactures against foodstuffs and raw materials....	100
	200

If trade does not balance, our method remains unchanged except for the addition of a new category, "exchange of commodities against invisible items," which accounts for the unbalanced part of trade. The following scheme would represent the normal case in which all categories of exchange are present:

SCHEME IV

	Imports	Exports
Foodstuffs and raw materials....................	75	30
Manufactured products	45	70
	120	100

According to our method, trade in this case can be subdivided as follows:

Exchange of commodities against "invisible items"............... 20
Exchange of foodstuffs and raw materials against foodstuffs and raw
    materials... 60
Exchange of manufactures against manufactures.................. 90
Exchange of manufactures against foodstuffs and raw materials...:. 50

        220

If there is a deficit (or surplus), trade obviously cannot consist only of the "traditional type of exchange." Thus, in the following example:

SCHEME V	Imports	Exports
Foodstuffs and raw materials....................	120	0
Manufactured products	0	100
	120	100

the total trade of 220 must be subdivided into two parts, 20, the exchange of goods against "invisible items," and 200, the "traditional type of exchange."

It remains, however, quite possible for the "traditional type of exchange" to shrink to zero. This happens whenever both commodity groups show a deficit (or a surplus), as in the following example:

SCHEME VI	Imports	Exports
Foodstuffs and raw materials....................	70	65
Manufactured products	50	35
	120	100

In this case the total trade is subdivided into:

Exchange of goods against "invisible items"..................... 20
Exchange of foodstuffs and raw materials against foodstuffs and raw
    materials.. 130
Exchange of manufactured products against manufactured products 70

        220

As we shall see, this pattern could actually be observed in a number of countries during recent years. It was characteristic of Italy for a long period running from 1892 to 1912. During this time Italy's trade balance was negative, not only as a whole, but also for the balances of all commodity groups taken separately. The opposite picture obtained for the foreign trade of the United States from 1898 to 1922. During this period, indeed, the United States foreign trade statistics show a surplus for each of the main commodity groups into which her foreign trade is subdivided.[3]

It is easy to give a more concrete meaning to the various categories of interchange in each particular case, as the compensated trade in a

---

[3] According to the national trade statistics of both the United States and Italy, which are both based upon a classification somewhat different from the Brussels classification.

commodity group is always obtained by doubling the smaller of the two opposite figures relating to imports and exports. Therefore, the exchange of manufactures against manufactures, for a country *having an active balance with respect to manufactures* (cf. Scheme IV), is a function of the *imports* of manufactures. But for a country having a passive balance in manufactures (cf. Scheme VI), the exchange of manufactures against manufactures is equal to twice the amount of the *exports* of manufactures.

Analogous meanings can be attached to the exchange of raw materials and foodstuffs according to whether the trade balance with respect to these two commodity groups is passive or active.

The exchange of manufactures against foodstuffs and raw materials, according to the case, is either *imports* of manufactures against *exports* of raw materials and foodstuffs or the opposite. Similarly, the exchange of commodities against "invisible items" stands either for a deficit or for a surplus of the trade balance.

The method which we have devised for the subdivision of the foreign trade of individual countries into the various categories of interchange can be applied to world trade as a whole. For this purpose we have to sum up by categories of interchange the results obtained in the analysis of the trade statistics of the individual countries, the values being expressed in an international currency.

Although an alternative approach to our problem might seem more natural at first sight, it is not of great value and little mention of it need be made. It consists in the division of countries into "industrial" and "raw material and foodstuff-producing" countries. Once this division is established, one might calculate the percentage in world trade of the interchange within "industrial" countries, within the "raw material and foodstuff-producing" countries, and between both groups of countries.[4]

It may be said generally that this method is inferior to the one proposed here, as a greater degree of abstraction is involved in labeling any given country as "industrial" than in labeling any given commodity as "manufactured." Thus, the interchange between industrial countries does not consist wholly of industrial products, nor does the interchange between industrial and agricultural countries consist exclusively of an interchange of manufactured products against foodstuffs. If a country having been predominantly "agri-

---

[4] This method has been applied by the *Institut für Weltwirtschaft* in its important inquiry into the structural changes of world economy (see below, pp. 127 f.).

cultural" comes to be predominantly "industrial," the dilemma arises whether to keep it in the class of "raw material and foodstuff-producing countries" or to transfer it to the "industrial countries." If the first course is adopted, the statistics become meaningless; if the second course is followed, their homogeneity is impaired. None of these difficulties is met with if our method is applied. All types of interchange are taken account of for every single country. And the industrialization of an agricultural country, which is evidently a gradual process, finds its expression in a gradual change in the importance of the various types of interchange for the foreign trade of this country.

Finally, we must warn the reader against a possible misinterpretation of the figures arrived at by our method. If we find, for instance, that the exchange of manufactures against manufactures for country A amounts to fifty million dollars, this does not necessarily mean that country A bought twenty-five millions of manufactures from countries B, C, and D and sold twenty-five millions of manufactures in exchange to these same countries. It might also mean that country A brought twenty-five millions of manufactures from countries B, C, and D and sold twenty-five millions of manufactures to countries E, F, and G. In other words, what we call exchange of manufactures against manufactures comprises not only the exchange of manufactures between industrial countries, but also an exchange of manufactures which is triangular with respect to countries. An example of this is Japan's traditional practice of offsetting imports of manufactures from the Western countries by exports of Japanese manufactures to Asia and Africa.

To this consideration the following corollary may be added: What we call the "traditional type of exchange," i.e., the exchange of manufactures against foodstuffs and raw materials, may be subdivided into two classes according to whether a country is exporting or importing manufactures against imports or exports of foodstuffs and raw materials. It is generally thought that the "industrial" or "agricultural" character of a country makes for a uniform structure of its foreign trade with all other countries, so that it exports manufactures to all of them and imports similarly foodstuffs and raw materials from all alike, or inversely. It is, however, quite possible for a country, such as Japan, to import raw materials (oil, tin, rubber) from one country (Dutch East Indies) against export of manufactures, and at the same time to export raw materials (silk) against import of manufactures from another country (United States). In this case the traditional type of exchange in the bilateral relations of Japan with the Dutch East Indies and the United States has the opposite sign. The amounts which thus cancel out are precisely the exchange of raw materials against raw materials and of manufactures against manufactures on a triangular basis, and only the balance, according to the meaning assigned to this term, constitutes a true exchange of manufactures against raw materials.[5] It would be very interesting to calculate subclasses of the various types of interchange according to whether they are bilateral or triangular with respect to countries; this would certainly bring out still better the complexity of international trade relations. Such an inquiry, however, would be feasible only if the trade statistics of the various countries were subdivided simultaneously according to both countries and to the Brussels commodity groups. To my knowledge Germany is the only country to have published this information.[6]

THE MAIN RESULT OF THE CALCULATIONS

By our calculations we have established for world trade as a whole the importance of the various types of interchange between groups of commodities. Although the compilation of this data was the most interesting feature of our calculations, the gathering of the necessary statistics was, however, by no means an easy matter. By drawing from various sources we have been able to find continuous and homogeneous series from 1925 to 1937 for forty-seven countries, accounting for approximately 92 per cent of world trade. The result for these forty-seven countries appears in table 11 (p. 151). But in table 3 we reproduce a slightly modified compilation for world trade as a whole which assumes a certain distribution of the trade not accounted for by the forty-seven countries.[7]

---

[5] See above, pp. 120–122.

[6] Cf. *Statistiches Jahrbuch* (Berlin, 1938), pp. 286–287.

[7] The only available basis for an international comparison is the already-quoted *International Classification of Brussels,* which was adopted in 1913. Many important countries, however, continued after that date to tabulate their trade statistics in a form more or less different from this classification. The *Bulletin du Bureau International de Statistique Commerciale* (Brussels, 1922, and following years), which was supposed to centralize the trade statistics tabulated according to the International Classifica-

For 1913, statistics for only twenty-two countries (73 per cent of world trade) could be collected. In order to obtain comparable figures for the years after the First World War, we have summed up the figures for the same countries for 1925 and 1929 (table 4).[8]

tion, carries a disappointingly small number of countries, many of which are quite unimportant. The best work in this field has been done by the German *Statistisches Reichsamt* which, in the absence of information in the national statistics, has itself carried out the calculations for a large number of countries. The results can be found in the successive editions of the *Statistisches Jahrbuch* (2d part, international tables) and in the *Statistisches Handbuch der Weltwirschaft* (Berlin, 1936). The data published by the *Statistisches Jahrbuch* are on the basis of a common currency (mark), which facilitated the calculation of totals for the world and various subgroups of countries. The information contained in the annual volumes of *International Trade Statistics* (ed. by the League of Nations) is either compiled from the national publications or from the German sources. In 1938 the *International Trade Statistics* dropped the tables giving the division of the trade according to the Brussels classification because of the adoption of a new international classification known as "minimum list." In the opinion of the author, the Brussels classification still fulfills a definite and valuable purpose and, rather than being entirely abandoned, it should be complemented.

The countries not included in the forty-seven countries for which complete statistics were available are some Asiatic (Formosa, Korea, Manchukuo) but mainly African and Latin American countries. The *Statistisches Jahrbuch* of 1938 carries for the first time detailed statistics for ten of these countries, accounting for approximately 5 per cent of world trade, and, as was to be expected, shows the share in total trade of the *exchange of manufactures against manufactures* to be much lower (only about 5 per cent) for these countries than for the forty-seven countries for which we had been able to collect continuous statistics. Therefore, we should have given too much importance to the exchange of manufactures against manufactures if we had simply assumed that the distribution of world trade according to the various types of interchange is the same as that found for the forty-seven countries. But the importance of the exchange of foodstuffs and raw materials against foodstuffs and raw materials in the total trade of the ten countries mentioned above was found to be approximately equal to that calculated for the forty-seven countries. In the estimate of the distribution of world trade, we have, therefore, proceeded in the following way:

(1) It was assumed that only 5 per cent of that part of world trade which was not accounted for by the trade of the forty-seven countries consisted in exchange of manufactures against manufactures.

(2) It was assumed that the percentage of the exchange of foodstuffs and raw materials against foodstuffs and raw materials remained for the world at the same figure which was calculated for the forty-seven countries.

(3) The exchange of commodities against invisible items of the balances of payments, being nothing but the sum of the deficits and surpluses of the individual trade balances, could be calculated without recourse to estimations, since complete statistics are available for the aggregate imports and exports of all countries.

(4) The exchange of manufactures against foodstuffs and raw materials is found as the balance of world trade and the three categories calculated according to the method just explained.

The possible range of error of the result seems, in this way, incapable of affecting any of the conclusions which we draw in the text.

[8] The countries are Germany, Belgium, Bulgaria, Denmark, France, Italy, Portugal, Rumania, Sweden, Spain, United Kingdom and Ireland, Russia, Tunisia, Egypt, Australia, India, China, Iran, Japan, United States, Canada, Peru. No account could be taken of frontier changes.

The striking fact which emerges from tables 3 and 4 is that the "traditional type of exchange," i.e., the exchange of manufactures against foodstuffs and raw materials, amounts only to somewhat less

TABLE 3

ESTIMATED PERCENTAGE DISTRIBUTION OF WORLD TRADE IN ACCORDANCE WITH THE VARIOUS TYPES OF INTERCHANGE

Year	(1)*	(2)†	(3)‡	(4)§	Total (5)
1925	13.9	39.6	17.2	29.3	100.0
1926	10.7	39.1	18.1	32.9	100.0
1927	11.7	38.7	18.9	30.7	100.0
1928	11.3	38.9	19.2	30.6	100.0
1929	9.3	38.3	19.4	33.0	100.0
1930	12.4	38.2	20.6	28.8	100.0
1931	16.5	37.1	21.5	24.9	100.0
1932	16.7	37.1	19.0	27.2	100.0
1933	15.6	36.5	18.7	29.2	100.0
1934	15.1	35.6	18.6	30.7	100.0
1935	13.7	36.0	18.1	32.2	100.0
1936	14.3	34.4	17.0	34.3	100.0
1937	14.7	34.8	17.2	33.3	100.0

* Exchange of commodities against "invisible items."
† Exchage of foodstuffs and raw materials against foodstuffs and raw materials.
‡ Exchange of manufactures against manufactures.
§ Exchange of manufactures against foodstuffs and raw materials.

TABLE 4

PERCENTAGE DISTRIBUTION OF THE TRADE OF TWENTY-TWO COUNTRIES IN 1913, 1925, AND 1929 IN ACCORDANCE WITH THE VARIOUS TYPES OF INTERCHANGE

Year	(1)*	(2)†	(3)‡	(4)§	Total (5)
1913	10.8	40.0	19.4	29.8	100.0
1925	12.5	39.2	19.7	28.6	100.0
1929	9.4	38.0	21.8	30.8	100.0

* Exchange of commodities against "invisible items."
† Exchage of foodstuffs and raw materials against foodstuffs and raw materials.
‡ Exchange of manufactures against manufactures.
§ Exchange of manufactures against foodstuffs and raw materials.

than one-third of total world trade. This is by no means a negligible proportion, but it is also far from occupying the dominating position often attributed to it. On the other hand, the opposite thesis, that trade is based largely upon the division of labor between national industries, is only partly verified by our figures. During the period under review, the exchange of manufactures against manufactures did not account for more than one-fifth or one-sixth of world trade. Instead, another category which is hardly ever mentioned in discussions about the structure of world trade takes on quite impressive proportions: the exchange of foodstuffs and raw materials against foodstuffs and raw materials. Being consistently the largest single item of the four classes into which we have subdivided world trade, it oscillates between two-fifths and one-third of the total.

It is instructive to compare our statistics with those compiled for a similar purpose by the Institut für Weltwirtschaft in Kiel showing

TABLE 5*

WORLD TRADE DIVIDED INTO TRADE BETWEEN VARIOUS TYPES OF COUNTRIES

Year	Foreign trade between "agricultural" countries	Foreign trade between "industrial" countries	Foreign trade between "agricultural" and "industrial" countries
1913	10.7	29.2	58.8
1925	11.5	25.0	62.2
1929	12.0	23.9	62.6

* From Institut für Weltwirtschaft und Seeverkehr, "Die Aussenhandelsentwicklung und das Problem der deutschen Ausfuhrpolitik," *Weltwirtschaftliches Archiv*, Vol. XXXVI (July, 1932), p. 34.

the respective importance in world trade of (1) the trade between agricultural countries, (2) the trade between industrial countries, and (3) the trade between agricultural and industrial countries. We reproduce in table 5 the findings of the Kiel Institute for 1913, 1925, and 1929.

These figures are instructive so far as they go. But they are entirely misleading if one equates "trade between industrial countries" with "exchange of manufactures against manufactures," "trade between agricultural and raw material-producing countries" with "exchange of foodstuffs and raw materials against foodstuffs and raw materials," and if one considers the trade between agricultural (and raw material-producing) countries and industrial countries as merely another expression for the exchange of foodstuffs and raw materials against manufactures. In 1929, for instance, the interchange between agricultural and raw material-producing countries amounted to 12.0 per cent of world trade, whereas the exchange of foodstuffs and raw materials against foodstuffs and raw materials amounted to 38.3 per cent—more than three times as much. The explanation of this discrepancy is, of course, that the trade between the industrial countries and between industrial and agricultural countries to a substantial extent consisted of an exchange of foodstuffs and raw materials against foodstuffs and raw materials. The figures of table 5 seem also to admit of the conclusion that the division of labor between the various national industries diminished continuously from 1913 to 1929.[9] Our data, on the contrary, show a continuous increase of the exchange of manufactures against manufactures for the twenty-two countries from 1913 to 1925 and 1929 (table 4) and also conspicuously for world trade as a whole from 1925 to 1929 (table 3). The apparent contradiction between the two series of figures is easily resolved. On the one hand, the decrease of the trade between industrial countries may have been due entirely to a decrease of the trade of raw materials and foodstuffs among them, and, on the other hand, the "agricultural" countries may have increased their export of manufactures among themselves or even to the "industrial" countries.

In any case, although the relative importance of the division of labor between the countries generally labeled as "industrial" diminished from 1913 to 1929, the relative importance of the division of labor between the manufacturing industries of the various nations increased. It is only the latter development which is significant for an appreciation of the chances of future development of international industrial specialization. If, as a whole, the percentage included under the exchange of manufactures against manufactures appears to be rather low, we must remember that manufactured products occupy less than 40 per cent of world trade, the rest being made up by raw materials and foodstuffs.

We can, indeed, combine fruitfully our table with the data covering the respective parts played in total world trade by manufactured products, foodstuffs, and raw materials. In table 3, column (2) refers exclusively to foodstuffs and raw materials, and column

---

[9] This conclusion, with its obvious pessimistic implications, has been drawn by the Institut für Weltwirtschaft und Seeverkehr, "Die Aussenhandelsentwicklung und das Problem de deutschen Ausfuhrpolitik," *Weltwirtschaftliches Archiv*, Vol. XXXVI (July, 1932), p. 34, and in a signed article by one of its authors; cf. Max Victor, "Das sogenannte Gesetz der abnehmenden Aussenhandelsbedeutung," *Weltwirtschaftliches Archiv*, Vol. XXXVI (July, 1932), p. 73.

(3) refers exclusively to manufactures. Column (4), showing the exchange of manufactures against foodstuffs and raw materials, includes equal amounts of both groups of commodities. Only for column (1)—the exchange of commodities against "invisible items"— do we not know the proportions of one or the other of the two commodity groups. But, knowing the total proportion in world trade of each group of commodities,[10] and the part played by each group in columns (2), (3), and (4) of table 3, we obtain the subdivision of our column (1) by subtraction. Thus we arrive at the conclusions presented in tables 6 and 7.

From these tables we see clearly the importance of the exchange of manufactures against manufactures. Though it represents not more than 17 to 19 per cent of total world trade (table 6), it has constituted *approximately one-half of the total trade in manufactures* throughout the period under consideration (table 7). Its importance with respect to the total trade in manufactures is thus only slightly smaller than the importance of the exchange of foodstuffs and raw materials against foodstuffs and raw materials within the total trade in these two groups of commodities.

DETAILED ANALYSIS OF THE STATISTICS FOR COUNTRIES AND GROUPS OF COUNTRIES

Before we proceed to the general significance of our statistical results, we must undertake a more detailed and rather tedious analysis. From table 3 the following main tendencies are apparent for the period under consideration (1925–1937):

1) The sums of the deficits and surpluses of commercial balances which represent the noncompensated commodity trade is subject to rather sudden change. The heavy contraction of trade accentuates the disequilibrium of nearly all trade balances. Only gradually is this disequilibrating effect of the crisis absorbed and, in 1937, the relative importance of what we have called the "exchange of commodities against invisible items" is still much higher than it was in 1929, though it does approach the 1925 figure.

---

[10] German statistics having provided the basis for the greater part of our calculations, these figures have also been calculated from a German source: *Statistisches Jahrbuch,* which gives detailed figures for world imports and world exports (e.g., *Jahrbuch,* 1938, p. 149). We have averaged the two figures and from this have obtained the percentages of table 6, which coincide with the data of the League of Nations' *Review of World Trade* (1938), p. 61. No data appear for the years from 1926 to 1928.

TABLE 6

Division of World Trade into Trade in Manufactures and Trade in Foodstuffs and Raw Materials, and Subdivision of Each Category into Various Types of Interchange

(in Percentage of World Trade)

	1925	1929	1931	1932	1933	1934	1935	1936	1937
World trade in foodstuffs and raw materials—Foodstuffs and raw materials exchanged against:									
Foodstuffs and raw materials*........	39.6	38.3	37.1	37.1	36.5	35.6	36.0	34.4	34.8
Manufactures†........	14.7	16.5	12.5	13.6	14.6	15.4	16.1	17.5	16.7
"Invisible items"‡........	9.9	5.8	10.1	11.5	11.3	10.7	10.0	11.0	11.0
Total foodstuffs and raw materials.....	64.1	60.6	56.6	62.2	62.4	61.6	62.1	62.5	62.4
World trade in manufactures—Manufactures exchanged against:									
Manufactures§........	17.2	19.4	21.5	19.0	18.7	18.6	18.1	17.0	17.2
Foodstuffs and raw materials†........	14.7	16.5	12.5	13.6	14.6	15.4	16.1	17.2	16.7
"Invisible items"‡........	4.1	3.5	6.5	5.2	4.3	4.5	3.7	3.4	3.8
Total manufactures........	35.9	39.4	40.4	37.8	37.6	38.4	37.9	37.5	37.6
Total world trade........	100.0	100.0	100.0	100.0	100.0	100.0	100.0	100.0	100.0

* Figures in this row correspond to those in column (2), table 3.
† Figures in these two rows correspond to those in column (4), table 3, divided by two.
‡ Figures in these two rows added together correspond to those in column (1), table 3.
§ Figures in this row correspond to those in column (3), table 3.

TABLE 7

DIVISION OF WORLD TRADE IN FOODSTUFFS AND RAW MATERIALS AND OF WORLD TRADE IN MANUFACTURES INTO VARIOUS TYPES OF INTERCHANGE

(in Percentage of Total World Trade in Foodstuffs and Raw Materials and Total World Trade in Manufactures)

	1925	1929	1931	1932	1933	1934	1935	1936	1937
World trade in foodstuffs and raw materials—Foodstuffs and raw materials exchanged against:									
Foodstuffs and raw materials.	61.8	63.2	62.2	59.6	58.5	57.8	58.0	55.0	55.8
Manufactures.	22.8	27.2	20.9	21.9	23.4	24.9	25.9	27.4	26.7
"Invisible items".	15.4	9.6	16.9	18.5	18.1	17.3	16.1	17.6	17.5
Total foodstuffs and raw materials.	100.0	100.0	100.0	100.0	100.0	100.0	100.0	100.0	100.0
World trade in manufactures—Manufactures exchanged against:									
Manufactures.	47.9	49.2	53.2	50.3	49.7	48.4	47.8	45.3	45.7
Foodstuffs and raw materials.	40.8	41.9	39.8	36.0	38.8	40.0	42.5	45.7	44.3
"Invisible items".	11.3	8.9	16.0	13.7	11.5	11.6	9.7	9.0	10.0
Total manufactures.	100.0	100.0	100.0	100.0	100.0	100.0	100.0	100.0	100.0

2) The exchange of foodstuffs and raw materials against foodstuffs and raw materials (or, as we shall call it also, the "compensated trade in foodstuffs and raw materials") exhibits a rather steady downward tendency.

3) The exchange of manufactures against manufactures (or the "compensated trade in manufactures") shows a steady increase in importance in each of the six years from 1925 to 1931, and a steady fall in the six following years, resulting in a figure for 1937 (17.2 per cent) exactly the same as the initial figure of the series.

As the data of table 4 show, however, there was a slight increase from 1913 to 1925 for the combined statistics of twenty-two countries, and the percentage included in this type of exchange in world trade was, for these countries, still greater in 1937 than it had been in 1913.

4) The movements of the exchange of manufactures against foodstuffs and raw materials are inversely related to the movements of the sum of deficits and surpluses. The share of the "traditional type of exchange" in world trade reaches its low point in 1931 (24.9 per cent) and from then on recovers speedily to a level even above its 1929 importance; it profits, indeed, from the concomitant fall of all other categories of interchange.

In order to explain these various movements, we return to the detailed statistics from which our aggregates have been compiled. From the standpoint of our analysis, it seems best to classify all countries into four groups or classes:

Class I.—Those which have an active balance in manufactures and a passive balance in foodstuffs and raw materials. The "traditional type of exchange" consists, therefore, for these countries in an export of manufactures against imports of foodstuffs and raw materials.

Class II.—Those which have a passive balance in manufactures and an active balance in foodstuffs and raw materials. The "traditional type of exchange" consists here of imports of manufactures against foodstuffs and raw materials.

Class III.—Those which have an active balance in both manufactures and in foodstuffs and raw materials.

Class IV.—Those which have a passive balance in both manufactures and in foodstuffs and raw materials. For the latter two classes of countries, the "traditional type of trade" is nonexistent, as we have shown above, page 121.

Obviously, the great majority of countries belong to the first two classes. The trade statistics of most countries show at least *some* of the "traditional type of exchange." Not a single country for the whole period under consideration belonged to Class III. The United States alone belonged to this class in 1913 and fell back into it in

1932 and 1933. During these depression years, the foodstuffs and raw materials balance became active once more because the imports had been reduced at a pace faster than that of the exports. The only other country in Class III is Hungary, which in 1937 fell for the first time into this class when her exports of manufactures slightly exceeded her imports.

Class IV is represented by four European countries, the Netherlands, Sweden, Greece, and Portugal, each of which have traditionally passive trade balances in manufactures as well as in foodstuffs and raw materials.[11] China also belongs to this category from 1930 to 1935, and other countries, Spain, Switzerland, Eire, and Norway, enter into it occasionally.

We have then only four countries for which the "traditional type of exchange" is consistently absent. Of the forty-three (or fifty-three) remaining countries, ten, generally termed "industrial," belong to Class I. These are the United States, England, Germany, France, Italy, Belgium, Austria, Czechoslovakia, Switzerland, and Japan. All other countries for which we have analyzed the trade statistics belong essentially to Class II.

If we compile separately the data for the ten countries belonging to Class I and for the thirty-three (or forty-three) countries belonging to Class II, the various types of interchange acquire a more concrete meaning. For the countries having an active balance in manufactures, the compensated trade in manufactures measures essentially the relative importance of the *imports* of manufactures, whereas for countries having a passive balance in manufactures, the compensated trade in manufactures is nothing but twice the percentage embraced by the *exports* of manufactures in the total trade of these countries.[12] The same applies, *mutatis mutandis,* to the compensated trade in raw materials and foodstuffs.

In table 8 statistics are given for the ten countries belonging to Class I and for the thirty-three countries belonging to Class II for 1925, 1929, 1931, and 1937. For 1929 and 1937 we were able to calculate statistics for ten additional countries belonging to Class II. Their inclusion does not alter substantially the picture given by the

---

[11] During the period under consideration this is true without exception for the Netherlands and for Portugal. Exceptions for Sweden and Greece are rare and insignificant.

[12] See above, p. 122.

figures for the thirty-three countries only. The ten countries of Class I and the forty-three countries of Class II account on the average for 55 and 35 per cent of world trade, respectively. The ten countries of Class I include the most important trading nations.

TABLE 8

PERCENTAGES HELD BY THE VARIOUS CATEGORIES OF INTERCHANGE IN THE TOTAL TRADE
OF DIFFERENT CLASSES OF COUNTRIES

	1925	1929	1931	1937
Exchange of commodities against "invisible items"				
Class I (10 "industrial" countries)............	11.9	10.0	17.2	13.9
Class II (33 "agricultural" countries).........	13.3	8.6	12.9	15.0
Class II (43 "agricultural" countries).........	....	8.9	....	15.5
Total (10 "ind." plus 33 "agr." countries).....	12.4	9.5	15.7	14.3
Total (10 "ind." plus 43 "agr." countries).....	....	9.6	....	14.5
Exchange of foodstuffs and raw materials against foodstuffs and raw materials:				
Class I (10 "industrial" countries)............	37.7	35.4	33.2	31.0
Class II (33 "agricultural" countries).........	40.1	40.7	41.4	37.4
Class II (43 "agricultural" countries).........	....	40.5	....	36.3
Total (10 "ind." plus 33 "agr." countries).....	38.6	37.3	36.0	33.3
Total (10 "ind." plus 43 "agr." countries).....	....	37.3	....	33.1
Exchange of manufactures against manufactures:				
Class I (10 "industrial" countries)............	21.1	24.3	27.3	20.2
Class II (33 "agricultural" countries).........	12.2	12.3	12.7	13.3
Class II (43 "agricultural" countries).........	....	11.7	....	12.3
Total (10 "ind." plus 33 "agr." countries).....	17.8	20.0	22.3	17.7
Total (10 "ind." plus 43 "agr." countries).....	....	19.5	....	17.1
Exchange of manufactures against foodstuffs and raw materials:				
Class I (10 "industrial" countries)............	29.3	30.3	22.3	34.9
Class II (33 "agricultural" countries).........	34.4	38.4	33.0	34.3
Class II (43 "agricultural" countries).........	....	38.9	....	35.9
Total (10 "ind." plus 33 "agr." countries).....	31.2	33.2	26.0	34.7
Total (10 "ind." plus 43 "agr." countries).....	....	33.6	....	35.3

In table 8 the figures for the forty-three (or the fifty-three) countries correspond both in their level and in their movements very closely to the results of table 3, which attempted an estimate for the whole of world trade. We can, therefore, explain the increasing and decreasing importance of the various types of interchange as shown in table 3 by reference to the present table.

The most striking result is the great discrepancy both in level and in movement which is revealed for the two groups of countries in the figures relating to the compensated exchange in manufactures. This type of interchange is nearly twice as important for the ten countries having an active balance in manufactures as for the thirty-three (or forty-three) countries having a passive balance in manufactures. In other words, imports of manufactures are much more important for the countries prevalently exporting manufactures than are the exports of manufactures for the countries prevalently importing manufactures. This result is not unexpected, and it is even surprising to note that, for the forty-three countries generally classified as "agricultural," the exchange of manufactures against manufactures still amounted to as much as 29 per cent of their total trade.

The more significant result is that these latter countries are characterized by a slow but continuous increase of the proportion in the total trade of the compensated trade in manufactures. This reflects the very gradual increase of their exports of manufactured products, in itself an outgrowth of the industrialization of these countries. On the other hand, the proportion in total trade of the compensated trade in manufactures changes very markedly for the ten countries having an active balance in manufactures. These changes dominate the movements of the total compensated trade in manufactures, since two-thirds to three-fourths of this total is handled by the ten industrial countries.

We may distinguish two periods from this angle. The first, extending from 1925 to 1931, is marked by an important increase in the part played by the compensated trade in manufactures in the total trade of the "industrial" countries. A subsequent strong decrease reduces the proportion of this type of trade below the initial percentage of 1925. Going back to the statistics of the individual countries, we find that most of them follow this same pattern. Germany and Japan, the only exceptions, have their maxima during 1927 and 1928, respectively. The peak in 1931 is explained by the relatively strong industrial exports of Germany which had a large active trade balance during this year. A considerable part of Germany's industrial exports goes traditionally to the other industrial countries. But, 1931 being the last free trade year for Great Britain, the substantial advance buying of manufactures carried the proportion of the compensated trade in manufactures in total British trade to an all-time high point of 33 per cent.

The subsequent decline of the compensated trade in manufactures is accompanied by a decline of the compensated trade in raw materials and foodstuffs, and the "traditional type of exchange" gains considerably in importance. Whereas the increase in world trade from 1925 to 1929 was marked by a more than proportional increase of the compensated exchange of manufactures, the short-lived revival of world trade after the great depression, with its intensified economic nationalism, witnessed a relative decline of this type of interchange.

The ten industrial countries also exhibit a continuous decline in the relative importance of the compensated exchange in raw materials and foodstuffs. This is tantamount to a decline in the relative importance of the *exports* of raw materials and foodstuffs in these countries, and it may be explained by their further industrialization and by the desire of Germany, Italy, and Japan to make the most of the natural resources within their own territories.

With respect to individual countries, the arrangement which we have devised for the analysis of total trade into the various types of interchange cannot add materially to the information contained in the traditional device of giving separate figures for imports and exports. But for an analysis from a certain standpoint it conveniently sums up the information contained in the ordinary arrangement.

For the larger industrial countries, such as the United States, Great Britain, France, Japan, and Italy, the proportion of the compensated trade in manufactures is generally somewhere between 20 and 25 per cent of total trade. It is distinctly lower for Germany.[18] Really high percentages can be found for such small industrial countries as Switzerland (49 per cent), Austria (32 per cent), Czechoslovakia (28 per cent), and for some countries having a passive balance in manufactures, such as Sweden (41 per cent), Netherlands (27 per cent), and even in some of the countries generally classified as "agricultural," such as China (33 per cent), Hungary (33 per cent),

---

[18] See below, pp. 137–138.

Canada (32 per cent), and India (31 per cent).[14] On the other hand, for a great number of "agricultural" countries the compensated trade in manufactures represents a very low proportion. For twenty-one of the thirty-three countries of Class II it did not exceed 5 per cent in 1937.

The proportion in total trade of the compensated trade in food-stuffs and raw materials is, on the contrary, much more steady from country to country. In 1937 it lies below 20 per cent of total trade for four countries only, Switzerland (13 per cent), Rumania (17 per cent), Turkey (16 per cent), and Netherlands Indies (14 per cent). There is a surprisingly large number of countries for which this type of trade represents more than or approximately one-half of total trade.[15]

These countries are not quite equaled with respect to aggregate importance by those the trade pattern of which is prevalently the exchange of manufactures against foodstuffs and raw materials.[16]

As to the movements of our figures for individual countries, the most interesting series is again the German one. In the first place, with the exception of the "rationalization" years of the 'twenties, the proportion of the compensated exchange of manufactures in German trade has always been by far the smallest of all the countries having an export surplus in manufactures. Furthermore, since Germany's commercial deficit was generally smaller than that of the other "industrial" countries, she carries on a larger amount of exchange of manufactures against foodstuffs and raw materials than these countries. Since 1933 the proportion of this type of exchange

---

[14] Parenthetical percentages here relate to 1937.

[15] These countries were in 1937: Spain (73 per cent), Greece (72 per cent), Poland (68 per cent), Eire (65 per cent), Denmark (62 per cent), British Malaya (60 per cent), Portugal (58 per cent), Netherlands (58 per cent), Hungary (57 per cent), Norway (54 per cent), United States (52 per cent), U. S. S. R. (52 per cent), Sweden (52 per cent), Belgium (49 per cent), Latvia (47 per cent), Tunisia (46 per cent). In light of these figures, the statement of Professor Howard S. Ellis (*Exchange Control in Central Europe* [Cambridge, Mass., 1941], p. 319) that "if autarky becomes universal, it would seem to imply the virtual cessation of international trade in finished goods and the reduction of trade in raw materials to the exchange of goods without close substitutes" is seen to be based on real possibilities. Cf., however, tables 1 and 2 for the tendency toward a decline of this type of interchange in world trade as a whole.

[16] Figures for 1937 are: Turkey (72 per cent), New Zealand (70 per cent), Germany (68 per cent), Bulgaria (64 per cent), Thailand (63 per cent), Rumania (69 per cent), Australia (58 per cent), Yugoslavia (58 per cent), Peru (57 per cent), Brazil (57 per cent), Belgian Congo (56 per cent), Egypt (53 per cent), Netherlands Indies (53 per cent), Lithuania (52 per cent), Argentina (52 per cent), Algeria (52 per cent).

increased further, from about one-half to two-thirds of Germany's total trade, due to the deliberate policy of the National Socialist government of restricting imports of manufactures and exports of raw materials and foodstuffs. Again, as in our analysis of the direction of German trade toward the smaller countries, we witness here a considerable change in the structure of German trade since 1933; and again this development can be viewed as an accentuation of previous tendencies.

The trade of Japan displays structural tendencies similar to those shown by the German trade. We note, indeed, a tendency toward a decrease of the compensated trade both in manufactures and in raw materials and foodstuffs. As a consequence, the importance of the "traditional type of exchange" increases sharply from one-fifth of total trade in the 'twenties to one-half in the 'thirties. Italian trade, on the contrary, does not share these movements.

In France one notices mainly a strong decrease in the importance of the "traditional type of exchange," explained partly by an increase in the compensated trade in manufactures but mainly by increase of "invisible items" of the balance of payments, i.e., by the rising deficit of French foreign trade.

Like Germany and Japan, the United States shows a decrease in the compensated trade in raw materials and foodstuffs, which, after having constituted about 70 per cent of total trade in 1925, declined to approximately 50 per cent in 1937. This development brought about an increase of the "traditional type of exchange," which is explained by the fact that the United States was still increasing the exports of manufactures at the expense of the exports of raw materials and foodstuffs without materially altering the structure of imports.

In the U. S. S. R. the most interesting development is the increase of the compensated trade in manufactures from 4.4 per cent in 1925 to between 20 and 30 per cent in the 'thirties. Because Russia has a passive balance in manufactures, the compensated trade in manufactures stands for exports of manufactures, and its increase shows the rising importance of Russian industrial exports.

In England there is from 1925 to 1931 a steady increase of the compensated trade in manufactures as a proportion of total trade. A sudden jump upward in 1931 brings this type of trade to 33 per cent of total trade.[17] Since, at the same time, the commercial deficit reaches a peak figure of 33 per cent of total trade, the "traditional type of exchange" shrinks in this year to one-sixth of total trade, a record low level. Subsequently, this type of trade recovers, but does not quite reach its former level. Answering to the new protectionist policy, the compensated trade in manufactures falls off decisively from 1931 to 1932 and maintains itself from then on at a level which is slightly lower than that reached in 1925. The relative magnitude of the deficit remains important throughout the 'thirties, whereas no particular change is noticeable for the compensated trade in raw materials and foodstuffs.

The general impression from our short survey of the trade statistics of individual countries is that no single pattern can describe the commodity structure of the foreign trade of all of them. The traditional conception that the exchange of manufactures against foodstuffs and raw materials is the backbone of foreign trade is verified only by a limited number of countries. At least as important are those countries the trade of which is in the main an exchange of foodstuffs and raw materials against foodstuffs and raw materials and those the trade of which is more or less equally subdivided into the various categories of interchange which we have here distinguished.

It is therefore also very difficult to point to any definite "law" according to which the commodity structure of foreign trade changes in the course of an economic development such as industrialization. This process does not necessarily lead to either a decrease of industrial imports or an increase of industrial exports, nor does it lead to either an increase of the imports or a decrease of the exports of raw materials. It is, however, likely to bring about at least one of these developments; and therefore the exchange of manufactures against foodstuffs and raw materials, which before the start of the process stands for imports of manufactures against exports of foodstuffs and raw materials, is likely to diminish and may even vanish in the first phase of industrialization and emerge with reversed conditions (exports of manufactures against imports of foodstuffs and raw materials) at a later stage. How far this development goes depends entirely on the particular country. It may even never come

---

[17] See above, p. 136.

TABLE 9

PERCENTAGE DISTRIBUTION OF THE TRADE OF SOME IMPORTANT COUNTRIES IN ACCORDANCE
WITH THE VARIOUS TYPES OF INTERCHANGE (1913-1937)

Year	(1)*	(2)†	(3)‡	(4)§	Total (5)
		GERMANY			
1913...................	3.2	32.2	13.3	51.3	100.0
1925...................	14.2	23.4	18.5	43.9	100.0
1926...................	1.1	28.5	13.8	56.6	100.0
1927...................	16.4	21.9	20.8	40.9	100.0
1928...................	9.3	22.9	19.9	48.7	100.0
1929...................	0.1	27.1	16.9	55.9	100.0
1930...................	7.4	26.7	16.0	49.9	100.0
1931...................	17.6	27.2	15.0	40.2	100.0
1932...................	10.3	24.0	14.0	51.7	100.0
1933...................	7.3	23.9	14.8	54.0	100.0
1934...................	3.3	21.2	17.4	58.1	100.0
1935...................	1.3	20.2	13.4	65.1	100.0
1936...................	6.1	18.3	11.7	63.9	100.0
1937...................	3.9	18.6	10.2	67.3	100.0
		JAPAN			
1913...................	7.3	65.3	18.4	9.0	100.0
1925...................	5.7	49.0	22.5	22.8	100.0
1926...................	9.2	45.6	24.0	21.2	100.0
1927...................	6.5	48.3	24.2	21.0	100.0
1928...................	5.6	49.4	26.0	19.0	100.0
1929...................	3.0	46.1	21.7	29.2	100.0
1930...................	3.5	41.3	20.7	34.5	100.0
1931...................	6.6	40.4	20.3	32.7	100.0
1932...................	3.7	37.8	17.6	40.9	100.0
1933...................	2.4	33.0	16.3	48.3	100.0
1934...................	3.2	26:9	15.8	54.1	100.0
1935...................	0.1	30.9	13.9	55.1	100.0
1936...................	0.8	30.5	12.4	56.3	100.0
1937...................	6.5	26.7	21.0	45.8	100.0

* Exchange of commodities against "invisible items."
† Exchange of foodstuffs and raw materials against foodstuffs and raw materials.
‡ Exchange of manufactures against manufactures.
§ Exchange of manufactures against foodstuffs and raw materials.

TABLE 9—(*Continued*)

Year	(1)*	(2)†	(3)‡	(4)§	Total (5)
			ITALY		
1913...................	18.4	55.7	25.9	....	100.0
1925...................	17.8	42.5	26.3	13.4	100.0
1926...................	13.2	34.8	25.0	27.0	100.0
1927...................	16.2	32.2	26.1	25.5	100.0
1928...................	20.1	37.3	29.3	13.3	100.0
1929...................	17.7	37.8	31.6	12.9	100.0
1930...................	17.7	39.8	33.2	9.3	100.0
1931...................	6.4	44.0	29.0	20.6	100.0
1932...................	9.5	45.3	29.3	15.9	100.0
1933...................	10.6	46.3	30.7	12.4	100.0
1934...................	18.8	42.3	31.1	7.8	100.0
1935...................	19.5	38.3	29.2	13.0	100.0
1936...................	4.2	47.7	28.2	19.9	100.0
1937...................	14.0	37.3	22.8	25.9	100.0
			FRANCE		
1913...................	10.1	35.2	21.7	33.0	100.0
1925...................	2.3	30.6	12.5	54.6	100.0
1926...................	0.3	31.8	13.2	54.7	100.0
1927...................	2.0	35.4	13.7	48.9	100.0
1928...................	1.5	31.1	19.1	48.3	100.0
1929...................	7.5	31.1	18.9	42.5	100.0
1930...................	10.2	30.0	26.4	33.4	100.0
1931...................	16.2	26.6	26.5	30.7	100.0
1932...................	20.4	26.1	23.5	30.0	100.0
1933...................	21.2	26.4	22.4	30.0	100.0
1934...................	12.8	31.1	21.6	34.5	100.0
1935...................	15.0	33.9	19.5	31.6	100.0
1936...................	24.3	31.8	18.8	25.1	100.0
1937...................	27.7	32.2	19.8	20.3	100.0

* Exchange of commodities against "invisible items."
† Exchange of foodstuffs and raw materials against foodstuffs and raw materials.
‡ Exchange of manufactures against manufactures.
§ Exchange of manufactures against foodstuffs and raw materials.

National Power and Foreign Trade

TABLE 9—(*Continued*)

Year	(1)*	(2)†	(3)‡	(4)§	Total (5)
	UNITED STATES				
1913.....................	15.9	64.7	19.4	....	100.0
1925.....................	7.6	69.7	20.3	2.4	100.0
1926.....................	3.1	64.4	22.3	10.2	100.0
1927.....................	6.4	64.4	23.4	5.8	100.0
1928.....................	11.5	64.7	22.9	0.9	100.0
1929.....................	8.9	59.2	23.8	8.1	100.0
1930.....................	11.5	61.8	22.5	4.2	100.0
1931.....................	7.6	60.6	24.8	7.0	100.0
1932.....................	10.1	65.6	24.3	....	100.0
1933.....................	7.3	69.1	23.6	....	100.0
1934.....................	12.5	66.0	20.9	0.6	100.0
1935.....................	4.8	59.1	20.7	15.4	100.0
1936.....................	0.1	52.1	21.4	26.4	100.0
1937.....................	4.5	52.3	19.4	23.8	100.0
	U. S. S. R.				
1913.....................	5.0	63.8	5.9	25.3	100.0
1925.....................	13.8	72.9	4.4	8.9	100.0
1926.....................	5.5	66.9	4.2	23.4	100.0
1927.....................	6.1	64.8	5.1	24.0	100.0
1928.....................	9.1	72.3	9.8	8.8	100.0
1929.....................	2.4	52.5	16.1	29.0	100.0
1930.....................	1.1	36.7	15.0	47.2	100.0
1931.....................	15.3	29.7	14.5	40.5	100.0
1932.....................	10.8	29.3	21.4	38.5	100.0
1933.....................	13.0	29.5	28.4	28.5	100.0
1934.....................	28.6	37.8	30.7	2.9	100.0
1935.....................	20.7	44.8	23.0	11.5	100.0
1936.....................	0.3	45.4	19.9	34.4	100.0
1937.....................	12.6	52.2	20.8	14.4	100.0

* Exchange of commodities against "invisible items."
† Exchange of foodstuffs and raw materials against foodstuffs and raw materials.
‡ Exchange of manufactures against manufactures.
§ Exchange of manufactures against foodstuffs and raw materials.

TABLE 9—(*Concluded*)

Year	(1)*	(2)†	(3)‡	(4)§	Total (5)
	UNITED KINGDOM				
1913...................	12.2	17.1	29.3	41.4	100.0
1925...................	20.3	17.8	22.1	39.8	100.0
1926...................	26.2	14.0	23.4	36.4	100.0
1927...................	21.4	17.8	24.2	36.6	100.0
1928...................	19.6	17.0	25.0	38.4	100.0
1929...................	20.7	18.1	25.5	35.7	100.0
1930...................	25.3	17.5	27.8	29.4	100.0
1931...................	34.2	16.3	33.0	16.5	100.0
1932...................	28.1	17.9	20.2	13.8	100.0
1933...................	26.0	19.0	19.6	35.4	100.0
1934...................	26.4	18.3	20.4	34.9	100.0
1935...................	24.4	19.3	20.6	35.7	100.0
1936...................	28.2	17.9	21.8	32.1	100.0
1937...................	29.3	17.8	21.3	31.6	100.0

* Exchange of commodities against "invisible items."
† Exchange of foodstuffs and raw materials against foodstuffs and raw materials.
‡ Exchange of manufactures against manufactures.
§ Exchange of manufactures against foodstuffs and raw materials.

about. Neither Sweden nor the Netherlands, even though they must be numbered among the industrialized nations, has reached the stage at which it exports manufactures against foodstuffs and raw materials. That the structure of the foreign trade of an old industrial country may be strongly affected by the industrialization of new countries we shall now show by reviewing the foreign trade of Great Britain during the nineteenth century.

THE COMMODITY STRUCTURE OF BRITISH FOREIGN TRADE SINCE 1854

In a recent valuable study the yearly foreign trade statistics of the United Kingdom have been subdivided into the commodity classes of the Brussels classification from 1814 on. Figures for exports and reëxports as well as for imports are, however, available only since 1854.[18]

---

[18] Werner Schlote, *Entwicklungen und Strukturwandlungen des englischen Aussenhandels von 1700 bis zur Gegenwart* (Probleme der Weltwirtschaft), Vol. 62 (Jena, 1938), pp. 125–132. This work points out (on pp. 11–13) the difference between the Brussels classification and the official Board of Trade classification. Schlote gives figures for

We have thought it interesting to summarize these statistics according to our method by distinguishing the various categories of interchange between commodity groups. Here again we must emphasize that we attribute to this method of presenting the statistics of an individual country no other intent or merit than to reveal at a glance the structural development of its foreign trade from a certain standpoint.

Ever since 1854 Britain has had an active balance in the trade in manufactured products, a passive balance in the trade in raw materials and foodstuffs, and a passive general balance of trade. Consequently, the meaning of the various categories of interchange is the following: The exchange of commodities against "invisible items" indicates the relative importance in the total turnover of trade of the goods imported, thanks to the active balance of the "invisible items." The exchange of foodstuffs and raw materials against foodstuffs and raw materials stands for the relative importance of twice the *exports* of raw materials and foodstuffs. The exchange of manufactures against manufactures indicates the importance in total trade of twice the *imports* of manufactures. And the exchange of manufactures against foodstuffs and raw materials stands obviously for *exports* of manufactures against *imports* of raw materials and foodstuffs. We have calculated the average percentages of these various categories for periods of ten years from 1854 to 1913. For the five years, 1925–1929, in order to bring about a higher degree of comparability with prewar figures, we give figures in which the political separation of Ireland from Great Britain is ignored.[19]

Table 10 brings out the fundamental change which has taken place in the structure of British foreign trade during the period under review. The outstanding fact is the decrease of the "traditional type of exchange"—the exchange of manufactures against foodstuffs and raw materials—from two-thirds of total trade to a proportion varying between one-third and two-fifths. This result is produced by the concomitant increase of all the other types of

general imports, special exports, and reëxports. To get figures for special imports, we have subtracted reëxports from general imports, and our method of subdividing trade into the various classes of interchange has then been applied to the figures for special imports thus found and to the figures for special exports directly given by Schlote.

[19] The basic figures are given by Schlote, *loc. cit.* See also *op. cit.*, pp. 40–41. For annual figures from 1925 to 1937 (excluding Eire), see table 9.

interchange, and is absolutely clear-cut until the decade 1894–1903. The increase in the share of the exchange of manufactures against manufactures is a particularly striking consequence of the "catching up" of countries like Germany and the United States, which sold increasing amounts of manufactured products on the English market. The increase of the compensated exchange in raw materials and foodstuffs, though less conspicuous, is important and interesting for a country so purely industrial as England. It is due mainly to

TABLE 10

PERCENTAGE DISTRIBUTION OF BRITISH FOREIGN TRADE IN ACCORDANCE WITH
VARIOUS TYPES OF INTERCHANGE (1854–1929)

Years	(1)*	(2)†	(3)‡	(4)§	Totals (5)	
					per cent	£
1854–1863...........	14.2	11.1	8.8	65.9	100.0	2,820,000,000
1864–1873...........	12.1	10.9	13.2	63.8	100.0	4,553,000,000
1874–1883...........	20.3	12.1	17.2	50.4	100.0	5,486,000,000
1884–1893...........	18.2	14.3	20.1	47.4	100.0	5,675,000,000
1894–1903...........	23.9	16.3	25.3	34.5	100.0	6,723,000,000
1904–1913...........	15.1	20.0	22.7	42.2	100.0	9,620,000.000
1925–1929...........	23.1	15.8	25.7	35.4	100.0	8,880,000,000

* Exchange of commodities against "invisible items."
† Exchange of foodstuffs and raw materials against foodstuffs and raw materials.
‡ Exchange of manufactures against manufactures.
§ Exchange of manufactures against foodstuffs and raw materials.

the increase of coal exports and of manufactured foodstuffs such as canned goods and beverages.

The increase of the "traditional type of exchange" from 1894–1903 to 1904–1913 is the consequence of a strong decrease in the relative—and absolute—magnitude of the commercial deficit. Again, this development is brought about by the favorable development of English exports in the decade preceding World War I. The slight decrease of the compensated trade in manufactures is more than offset by the continuing increase in the compensated trade in raw materials and foodstuffs. It should be noted that the proportion of imports of manufactures in total *imports* decreased only slightly (from 20.5 per cent in 1894–1903 to 19.7 per cent in 1904–1913), while increasing substantially in absolute terms. The somewhat greater falling off of the compensated trade in manufactures as a percentage in total imports *and* exports in the same period is explained by the increase in total exports relatively to total imports.

In 1925–1929 the distribution of British trade according to the various types of interchange had reverted very nearly to the pattern of 1894–1903.

Thus, we see that toward the end of the nineteenth century the structure of British foreign trade had become much more complex than it had been fifty years earlier. The statement that British trade consisted mainly in exports of manufactures against imports of foodstuffs and raw materials was still a valid generalization for the period 1854–1863. For the decade 1894–1903 it had become a distortion of the facts.

HISTORICAL IMPORTANCE OF THE TRADITIONAL VIEW OF THE COMMODITY STRUCTURE OF WORLD TRADE

Our calculations for world trade as a whole show that the traditional view that world trade is based primarily upon the exchange of manufactures against foodstuffs and raw materials is not even approximately correct. The preceding statistical analysis has brought out the importance of two additional types of the international division of labor, one consisting in an exchange of certain foodstuffs and raw materials against other foodstuffs and raw materials, and the other the exchange of manufactures against manufactures.

Our finding refutes the idea that the division of labor between industrial and agricultural countries is the only possible economic basis for the expansion of world trade. This belief has found its most articulate expression in the so-called "law of the declining importance of export trade" which Sombart formulated at the beginning of the century. Sombart claimed that the gradual industrialization of the agricultural countries would lead to a reduction of the growth of foreign trade with respect to the growth of internal trade and production.[20] But Sombart's "law" prophesied only a relative decline of foreign trade and was therefore a rather modest expression of a preoccupation which pervaded Germany at the turn of the century. At that time Germany had become a predominantly industrial nation, and the realization of this fact brought about a growing fear of Germany's dependence on foreign countries. This fear,

[20] Werner Sombart, *Die deutsche Volkswirtschaft im neunzehten Jahrhundert*, Chap. XIV (Berlin, 1903). In addition to the industrialization of agricultural countries, Sombart adduced as a reason for his forecast the increasing capacity to consume on the part of the home market.

which, curiously enough, coincided with the first wave of alarm in England and France over the advances of German industrial exports, had several origins. Germany was, of course, apprehensive of being shut off from her food and raw material supply in wartime. But increasing difficulties attending exports and, consequently, imports were feared even for peaceful times.

Germany looked at the rising American industries and at the growth of manufacturing in Russia and Italy and other "new" countries with much the same alarm as England looked at German competition. Let us quote one particularly naïvely concise expression of this alarm:

America wants to sell not only bread to Europe, but also everything else by the sale of which Europe could buy bread for herself. America wants to sell not only to Europe, but also to all the other countries buying now from Europe so that eventually Europe will have nothing left with which to pay for the bread. Such a state of affairs is of course bound to lead one day to a big catastrophe.[21]

In addition, the possibility of an abandonment of free trade by Great Britain was a constant preoccupation of German governments. But if one accepts the view that world trade can be based only upon the exchange of manufactures against foodstuffs and raw materials, then any springing up of new industries in "agricultural" countries, whether nurtured by tariffs or not, would endanger the export possibilities of the old industrial nations.

In part, the "terror of becoming a predominantly industrial state"[22] had origins of a social and military order. But economically it was the outcome of another "terror," the industrialization of the rest of the world, which, it was thought, would soon deprive Germany of her markets abroad. Thus, in the minds of the public and of many economists, the increasing importance of German foreign trade was coupled with an increasing precariousness of its economic basis. These views furnished one of the main arguments for the stepping up of agricultural protection under the Chancellorship of

---

[21] Emil Schalk, *Der Wettkampf der Völker mit besonderer Bezugnahme auf Deutschland und die Vereinigten Staaten von Amerika* (Jena, 1905), p. 53. Against these "theories," see the writings of one of the lone defenders of free trade in Imperial Germany, Karl Dietzel, *Der deutsch-amerikanische Handelsvertrag und das Phantom der amerikanischen Industriekonkurrenz* (Berlin, 1903), *Ist Maschinenausfuhr wirtschaftlicher Selbstmord?* (Berlin, 1907).

[22] Ludwig Brentano, *Die Schrecken des überwiegenden Industriestaates* (Berlin, 1901).

Bülow.[23] The policy of agricultural protection could, indeed, be considered as insurance against the day which would see the cessation of industrial exports and, consequently, of agricultural imports.

It was believed, however, that there was a possibility of preventing the collapse of foreign trade, either by obtaining sufficient colonies or, directly, by preventing the industrialization of foreign nations. Because of the increasing industrialization of other countries, particularly the United States, Russia, Japan, and India, the argument was made that the only means of obtaining future outlets for German industrial exports would be by an extension of German territory abroad. For this, in order to obtain and to hold colonies, a strong fleet was indispensable. This reasoning can be found repeatedly in a collection of essays in 1900 by German economists trying to convince the public of the necessity of naval armaments.[24] The alarm cry, "export or die," is one of the many slogans which Hitler did not invent. At the turn of the century, when Germany first realized her growing dependence on foreign countries, this cry was heard continuously. By the foregoing reasoning it was turned into "build a fleet or die," without, however, being drawn to its ultimate gloomy and somewhat paradoxical consequence, which would be "wage a war or die."

There is evidence that the fear of the ultimate collapse of foreign trade inspired also a more direct policy: the attempt to prevent the industrialization of other countries. Here we must again refer to Viner's statement that predatory dumping, i.e., dumping with the intent of crushing foreign industry, has been practiced by Germany on a larger scale than by any other country, particularly in Italy.[25]

The monopoly of the German chemical industry before World War I is a well-known fact. Accusations similar to those heard recently were voiced in 1917 in the United States by Secretary of Commerce W. C. Redfield. He said: "When peace shall come . . . it will hardly be said again to any Secretary of Commerce of the United

---

[23] Alexander Gerschenkron, *Bread and Democracy in Germany* (Berkeley, 1943), pp. 60–61.

[24] Paul Voigt, "Deutschland und der Weltmarkt," in *Handels- und Machtpolitik*, Vol. I (Stuttgart, 1900), pp. 196 ff.; also, Max Sering, "Die Handelspolitik der Grossmächte und die Kriegsflotte," *op. cit.*, Vol. II, pp. 32 ff.

[25] See above, pp. 55 f.

States that the German Dyestuff Verein will not 'permit' the establishment of an American dyestuff industry."[26] The Russians likewise complained that the commercial treaty which was imposed on them in the critical year 1904 contained, not only very high German tariffs against the Russian agricultural exports, but also very low Russian tariffs for industrial imports from Germany, so that Russian "infant industries" suffered from a continuous undernourishment.

I do not wish to imply that the policy of trying to prevent industrialization was as integral a part of German foreign economic policies before the First World War as it has been recently. But attempts in this direction certainly existed, and they were sufficient to arouse widespread apprehension and national resentment abroad. Often the setting up of German industries abroad was construed simply as an attempt by Germany to supervise the industrialization of other countries when she was unable to prevent it entirely.[27]

Thus, the mistaken idea that German foreign trade was threatened with collapse if the agricultural countries became industrialized had most serious consequences for peaceful international relations. Anticipation of this development produced a weighty argument for agricultural protection, whereas simultaneous efforts to stave it off contributed to the policy of naval armaments and led to a first attempt on the part of Germany to shape the economic development of other sovereign countries. All these policies of Imperial Germany have been carried forward by the National Socialist government.

We do not suggest that the traditional concept of the commodity-structure of world trade is alone responsible for the emergence of these policies. Considerations of economic and political power would amply warrant an attempt to prevent the industrialization of agricultural countries; and, from the purely economic standpoint, it is also understandable that German industries tried to bar the establishment of possible competitors abroad. The policy of agricultural protection and naval armaments can also be explained in

---

[26] Speech of October 16, 1917, quoted from Bureau of Foreign and Domestic Commerce, *German Trade and the War* (Washington, 1918), p. 15; cf. also the preface of A. Mitchell Palmer, wartime United States Alien Property Custodian, *in* Stanley Frost, *Germany's New War Against America* (New York, 1919).

[27] Cf. Henri Hauser, *Les méthodes allemandes d'expansion économique* (Paris, 1915), (English translation, *Germany's Commercial Grip on the World* [New York, 1917]), pp. 250–251. Also see above, p. 56.

terms of class or national power interests. The traditional view of the commodity-structure of world trade may then be considered as a rationalization of these interests in terms of economic analysis. But undoubtedly this very rationalization gave an added weight and impetus to their pursuit.

If we refer to a historical parallel, we may say that it would certainly be wrong to regard mercantilist views on the balance of trade as entirely responsible for the aggressive commercial policies of the seventeenth and eighteenth centuries. But supposed interests play their part in shaping actions, and economic theories play their part in creating interests. In this sense both the mercantilist theory of the balance of trade and the idea that world trade can only be based upon the division of labor between industrial and agricultural countries had a disruptive effect on international economic and political relations.

Any future reconstruction of world trade should take into account the complexity of its structure which our statistics reveal. On the one hand, it is certainly necessary to eradicate the attitude of many nations which feel degraded if they do not produce their own refrigerators and their own automobiles. But it is equally important for the industrial nations not to feel alarmed at the establishment of any new industry in any country classified as "agricultural."

We have touched here upon this feeling of alarm and its consequences only so far as Germany is concerned. But it has been a feature of all countries which have arrived at industrial maturity. An ancient statute, more honored by the breach than by observance, prohibiting the export of machinery was repealed in England a century ago. But the old belief that exports of this category means political and economic suicide for the "old" countries has never been abandoned, in part, we suspect, because it reintroduces the classical element of tragic fatality into modern life. The policy of all countries during the period of mercantilism was to prevent the spreading out of their particular skills and industrial arts. But this vestige of mercantilism has assumed a most beguiling disguise—that of the maintenance of a "sound" international division of labor.

An encouraging aspect of present thought on postwar reconstruction is therefore the radical change from the traditional outlook in this respect. Today, schemes for the future industrialization of underdeveloped countries, such as China and those in southeastern Europe, are proposed and discussed in many quarters; and the future economic mission of the older industrial countries is conceived less as the mechanical workshop of the world than as the initiator and educator in industrial processes.

International trade has nothing to fear from these developments, since there will probably always remain a fruitful division of labor

TABLE 11

PERCENTAGE DISTRIBUTION OF THE TOTAL TRADE OF FORTY-SEVEN COUNTRIES IN ACCORDANCE WITH THE VARIOUS TYPES OF INTERCHANGE (1925–1937)

Year	(1)*	(2)†	(3)‡	(4)§	Total (5)
1925	12.6	39.6	18.2	29.6	100.0
1926	10.7	39.1	19.2	31.0	100.0
1927	11.6	38.7	19.9	29.8	100.0
1928	11.5	38.9	20.4	29.2	100.0
1929	9.7	38.3	20.5	31.5	100.0
1930	12.5	38.2	21.7	27.6	100.0
1931	15.9	37.0	22.7	24.4	100.0
1932	15.5	37.1	20.1	27.3	100.0
1933	14.8	36.5	20.0	28.7	100.0
1934	15.0	35.7	19.8	29.5	100.0
1935	13.0	.36.0	18.7	32.3	100.0
1936	13.7	34.4	18.3	33.6	100.0
1937	14.1	34.7	18.5	32.7	100.0

* Exchange of commodities against "invisible items."
† Exchange of foodstuffs and raw materials against foodstuffs and raw materials.
‡ Exchange of manufactures against manufactures.
§ Exchange of manufactures against foodstuffs and raw materials.

between the various countries and parts of the world. But it is highly improbable that any *particular* pattern of the international division of labor will last forever. The transition from one pattern to another will certainly involve the drying up of certain types of commodity flows and the opening up of new types. Such a transition will present many adjustment difficulties which might best be solved by the establishment and extension of effective international controls. But to conclude that world trade is doomed because the traditional pattern of the international division of labor seems imperiled is one of these flights of the imagination at the start of which we find a lack of real imagination: an incapacity to conceive of a state of affairs radically different from that with which we have been acquainted.

APPENDIXES

APPENDIX A

Note on Statistical Methods

The index of preference for small trading countries (Chapter V).—According to the notation adopted on page 87 and following, we have three series:

1) The total amounts of exports of the various countries with which X trades, denoted by $E_1, E_2, \cdots, E_n$;

2) The various amounts of imports taken by country X from these countries, denoted by $i_1, i_2, \cdots, i_n$;

3) The ratios of percentages resulting from the division of the elements of series (2) by the elements of series (1) denoted by $\dfrac{i_1}{E_1}, \dfrac{i_2}{E_2}, \cdots, \dfrac{i_n}{E_n}$.

In order to study the preference of X's imports for small trading countries, we are interested, not in the correlation between series (1) and (2), which is almost certain to be positive, but in the correlation between series (1) and (3). The coefficient of correlation for these two series can be written, according to the product-moment formula, as follows:

(a)
$$r = \frac{\sum_{K=1}^{n} (E_K - M_E)\left(\dfrac{i_K}{E_K} - M_{i/E}\right)}{n \cdot \sigma_E \cdot \sigma_{i/E}}$$

where M_E is the arithmetic mean of series (1) and σ_E its standard deviation, and where $M_{i/E}$ is the arithmetic mean (unweighted average) of the ratios composing series (3) and $\sigma_{i/E}$ their standard deviation.

By multiplying by $\sigma_E \cdot \sigma_{i/E}$ and developing the right side, we obtain:

(b)
$$r \cdot \sigma_E \cdot \sigma_{i/E} = M_i - M_E \cdot M_{i/E}$$

where M_i is the arithmetic mean of country X's imports from the various countries [series (2)].

Introducing the coefficients of variation

$$v_E = \frac{\sigma_E}{M_E} \qquad\qquad Iv_{i/E} = \frac{\sigma_{i/E}}{M_{i/E}}$$

and dividing by $M_E \cdot M_{i/E}$, expression (b) gives

$$r \cdot v_E \cdot v_{i/E} = \frac{M_i}{M_E \cdot M_{i/E}} - I$$

[155]

(c)
$$\therefore \frac{M_{i/E}}{\dfrac{M_i}{M_E}} = \frac{1}{1 + r \cdot v_E \cdot v_{i/E}}$$

The left side of this equation is the quotient of the unweighted and the weighted average of the ratios acquired by country X in the exports of its trading partners; or, in other words, it is the average of the ratios divided by the ratio of the averages. The index of preference for small countries calculated by us is nothing but this expression multiplied for convenience by 100. The right side of the expression contains the justification of the index. By r we have expressed the correlation between the trade totals of the various countries and the percentages acquired in these totals by the trade of country X. The index of preference is therefore equal to 100 where there is no correlation; it is superior to 100 when the correlation is negative (high percentages associated with small trade totals); and it is inferior to 100 when the correlation is positive.

The value of r determines, therefore, whether the preference of a country's trade is on the whole for the large or for the small trading countries, and it also determines the strength of this preference. The presence in our formula of the two coefficients of variation, however, means that, with a given positive (or negative) value of r, the preference for large (or small) trading countries increases with the relative dispersion of the two series. That this is fully justified, given the phenomenon we want to measure, may easily be seen by supposing that country X trades only with two countries of unequal size; then, the value of r is necessarily ± 1, provided only that the value of the two percentages or of the two export totals is not the same (then, r would be 0). But the preference for the large or the small trading countries is the more pronounced the greater the difference between the two percentages acquired in the trade of the two countries and also the greater the difference between the volumes of total trade of the two countries with which X trades. The first point is obvious, and the validity of the second becomes clear if we consider that our phenomenon increases also when, with an unchanged distribution of X's trade, the trade totals of its trading partners change so as to make the small trading countries smaller and the large trading countries still larger.

The fact that, in addition to r, our expression contains only the two coefficients of variation shows that our index is a pure number having no reference to any unit of measurement. This would not have been true if we had formed the difference instead of the quotient of the weighted and unweighted averages.[1]

---

[1] This difference could have been formed by dividing equation (b) above by M_E only. We would then have obtained an expression which is due to Karl Pearson, the derivation of which may be found in G. U. Yule and M. G. Kendall, *An Introduction to the Theory of Statistics* (London, 1940), pp. 302–304.

Our measure should be capable of rendering services in the measurement of similar phenomena in economic and demographic statistics. Thus, for instance, the attraction of certain sections of the population according to religion, profession, etc., to small or large cities could be measured in similar ways.

The index of concentration (Chapter IV).—The statistical treatment of the concept of concentration is historically connected with the measurement of income concentration. Some indices devised for this purpose,

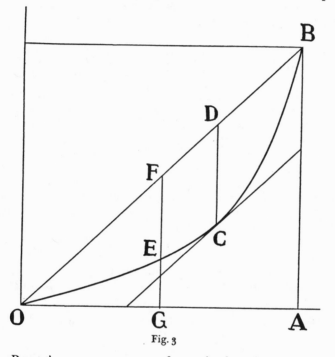

Fig. 3

such as Pareto's, are parameters of certain functions describing the income distribution. Among the devices which, on the contrary, are independent of the particular function to which the income distribution might be fitted, the best known is the Lorenz curve which, as has been shown mainly by Italian statisticians, is closely connected with the various measures of relative dispersion.[2]

---

[2] In figure 3, OCB is the Lorenz curve and OB the equidistribution line, i.e., the line with which the Lorenz curve would coincide if there were no concentration. The length of OA and of AB is unity. Then, if we draw a line vertically through the midpoint (G) of OA, the segment FE of this line contained between the Lorenz curve and the equidistribution line is half the quotient of the mean deviation from the median and the mean. If we draw a parallel to the equidistribution line so as to make it tangential to the Lorenz curve and draw a vertical line through the point of tangency C, the segment CD of this line is equal to half the quotient of the mean deviation from the

Concentration of income and inequality of distribution of income are one and the same thing. The number of income receivers is irrelevant for the concept of income concentration, as has been stated explicitly by D. B. Yntema in a study of the various indices proposed.[3] In various instances, however, the number of elements in a series the concentration of which is being measured is an important consideration. This is so whenever concentration means "control by the few," i.e., particularly in connection with market phenomena. Control of an industry by few producers can be brought about by inequality of distribution of the individual output shares when there are many producers or by the fact that only few producers exist. One of the well-known conditions of perfect competition is that no individual seller should command an important share of the total market supply; this condition implies the presence of both relative equality of distribution *and* of large numbers. The notion of concentration which one has in mind when speaking of industrial concentration is thus seen to be more complex than the concept of income concentration. Therefore, the methods which have been devised to measure the concentration of income are inadequate for the measurement of the concentration phenomenon with which we are here concerned. An extreme case is this: If we would try to read off from a Lorenz graph the degree of concentration of an industry in which two firms divided between themselves the total output, we would have to conclude that, because the Lorenz curve would coincide with the equidistribution line, there is no concentration.[4]

Concentration of control or of power over a corporation, over the market in one industry, or over foreign trade is not only a direct function of the relative inequality of distribution or dispersion, but also a reciprocal function of the number of stockholders, of producing firms in the industry, and of importing and exporting countries.

mean and the mean. Finally, the area bounded by the Lorenz curve and the equidistribution line, if divided by the triangle OAB, can be shown to result in the quotient of the "mean difference" and the mean. The "mean difference" is a measure of dispersion proposed by Corrado Gini; it consists in the average of all the differences which can be formed between the elements of a statistical series. The easy proofs of these theorems can be found in Gini, "Sulla misura della concentrazione e sulla variabilità dei caratteri," *Atti del R. Instituto Veneto di Scienze, Lettere e Arti,* Vol. LXXIV, Part II (1913–1914), pp. 1229–1233, and Gaetano Pietra, "Delle relazioni fra gli indici di variabilitá," *op. cit.,* Vol. LXXIV, Part II, pp. 775–784.

[3] D. B. Yntema, "Measures of the Inequality in the Personal Distribution of Wealth and Income," *Journal of the American Statistical Association,* Vol. 28 (December, 1933), p. 423.

[4] This shortcoming of the Lorenz curve has been recognized in Monograph No. 30 of the *Temporary National Economic Committee,* "Survey of Shareholdings in 1710 Corporations with Securities Listed on a National Securities Exchange" (Washington, 1941), page 48, note 3. As a remedy the authors propose to add to the Lorenz curve "a second and entirely independent figure, the reciprocal of the number of shareholders." This cumbersome procedure would be rendered unnecessary by the adoption of an index taking into account both factors upon which concentration depends.

As an index meeting these two requirements, we propose the square root of the sum of the square of the elements in the series when these elements are expressed as percentages of their sums.

If $a_1, a_2, \cdots, a_k, \cdots, a_n$ are the elements of an ungrouped statistical

series, and if we have $\sum\limits_1^n a_K = A$, then the index is

$$C = \sqrt{\sum_1^n \left(\frac{a_K}{A} \cdot 100\right)^2} = \frac{100}{A}\sqrt{\sum_1^n a_K{}^2}$$

To prove that this index fulfills the two requirements outlined above, we shall develop the standard deviation of the series, the arithmetic mean

of which is equal to $\dfrac{A}{n}$.

$$\sigma = \sqrt{\frac{\sum\limits_1^n \left(a_K - \dfrac{A}{n}\right)^2}{n}}$$

Squaring and multiplying by n,

$$n\sigma^2 = \sum_1^n \left(a_K - \frac{A}{n}\right)^2 = \sum_1^n a_K{}^2 - \frac{A^2}{n}$$

Dividing by $\dfrac{A^2}{n}$, and rearranging, we have

(1)
$$\frac{\sigma^2}{\dfrac{A^2}{n^2}} + 1 = \frac{n}{A^2} \cdot \sum_1^n a_K{}^2$$

In order to compare the dispersions of series with different arithmetic means, one uses the coefficient of variation

$$v = \frac{\text{standard deviation}}{\text{mean}}$$

Therefore, by substituting in (1)

$$v = \frac{\sigma}{\dfrac{A}{n}} \quad \text{and} \quad C = \frac{100}{A}\sqrt{\sum_1^n a_K{}^2}$$

we may write $v^2 + 1 = \dfrac{n}{100^2} \cdot C^2$

(2)
$$\therefore C = 100\sqrt{\frac{v^2 + 1}{n}}$$

This result shows clearly that the two conditions which any index of our concept of concentration should meet are fully realized by the measure here proposed: It increases with the relative dispersion v and decreases with the number n of the elements of the series.

Objection might be raised that any number of indices satisfying the two conditions could be devised and that the adoption of our index could only be the result of an arbitrary choice. Our reply is that it has always been the problem of descriptive statistics to-substitute some specific algebraic function for a broad type of "behavior" required by the characteristics of the phenomenon which is to be measured. The choice of the specific function is generally made on grounds of simplicity, intelligibility, expediency, or connection with mathematical statistics. All these reasons favor the adoption of our index:

1) it is directly and simply related to the standard deviation which, for the very reasons just stated, is the most generally accepted measure of dispersion;

2) it evolves, as was shown above (p. 156), from 0 to 100, a clear advantage for the interpretation of the various values of the index;

3) the index is easily intelligible and readily calculable. The series the concentration of which we want to measure is often given in percentage form already in the statistical source material (as, e.g., in the statistics relating to the distribution of foreign trade according to countries of destination and origin). If this is so, the computation of our index is considerably easier than that of the standard deviation, as all one has to do is to square the percentages and extract the square root from the sum of the squares.

Applications of the index of concentration to grouped or incomplete data.—A final advantage of the index is that it is applicable to grouped or incomplete data. In problems of geographical concentration, e.g., concentration of resources, of production, and of foreign trade according to countries, it is often possible to know the distinct value of every single item entering into the distribution. As to industrial concentration, the hearings before the Temporary National Economic Committee have disclosed some of the production data for single firms in certain branches of industry, e.g., the petroleum industry. But, generally, data relating to activities of single firms or corporations are withheld from the public, and special precautions are often taken to this end in presenting the statistics.[5] But even when no individual data are accessible the application of the index is possible when somewhat detailed frequency distributions are available. These distributions give for definite asset classes the number of enterprises and the amount of assets. Assuming equal distri-

[5] In the statistics of income of corporations, two income groups are classed together whenever in one class there is only one corporaton. For an analogous precaution, see National Resources Committee, *The Structure of the American Economy*, Part I (Washington, 1939–1940), p. 262.

bution within the frequency classes—the same assumption is implied when in a Lorenz graph one draws a straight line from one known point to the next. It is thus possible to give definite values to every single item through dividing the amount of assets by the number of enterprises to which they belong.

This procedure of course entails a certain amount of error (the narrower the frequency classes, the less this error will be), but this error is limited and is always in the same direction, since the value of the index will naturally always be lower than it would have been had the exact value of the single items been known.

It sometimes happens that we know in a series the individual sizes of the largest items, the rest being lumped together under the heading "other firms," "other countries," etc. In this also the approximate determination of the value of the index remains feasible, and we can even set a maximum and minimum limit to its possible values. Let us suppose that the four largest producers in an industry account for 40, 25, 10, and 5 per cent, respectively, of the total output, "other firms" producing the remaining 20 per cent. Then the index of concentration will be

$$\sqrt{1600 + 625 + 100 + 25 + p} = \sqrt{2350 + p},$$

p standing for the sum of the squares of the remaining items. The value of p depends on the size of these items; and, as no item may be larger than 5, the smallest of the four largest percentages, the upper limit for p is $4 \times 5^2 = 100$. The lower limit for p is o, which is approached as we assume the remaining items always to be smaller in size and larger in number. If we know the number of the remaining items, the lower limit rises to the value given by the assumption of no dispersion, i.e., of equality of all items. Thus, if the remaining items, making up a total of 20 per cent, are ten in number, the lower limit for p would be $10 \times 2^2 = 40$.

In other words, as was to be expected, the upper limit of p increases with the size of the percentage to be accounted for by the remaining items (let us call it k). But it is of interest to note that this upper limit depends, furthermore, on the size of the smallest of the known items, whereas the lower limit depends on the number of the remaining items and, given constant finite numbers, increases with k. It is thus seen that an increase of k does *not* lead necessarily to a widening of the limits and to a greater uncertainty concerning the value of the concentration index. This is shown by the following example:

	Industry 1	Industry 2
Largest producer	40	30
Second largest producer . . .	25	20
Third largest producer . . .	10	17
Fourth largest producer . . .	5	3
Twenty remaining items . . .	20	30
	100	100

Sum of squares of detailed items	2350	1598
Upper limit of sum of squares of undetailed items	100	90
Lower limit of sum of squares of undetailed items	20	45
Index of concentration as a mean of its upper and lower limit, with indication of limits . .	49.1 ± 0.4	40.8 ± 0.3

This example shows also that even when an apparently large percentage is left undetailed by the statistical data, a rather narrow circumscription of the value of the concentration index may still be possible.

Resolutions of the Paris Economic Conference of the Allies, June, 1916

WE HAVE QUOTED (on pp. 60–61) the preamble to the Paris Resolutions. The following is the text of the resolutions pertaining to postwar economic policy.[1]

B

TRANSITORY MEASURES FOR THE PERIOD OF COMMERCIAL, INDUSTRIAL, AGRICULTURAL, AND MARITIME RECONSTRUCTION OF THE ALLIED COUNTRIES

I

The Allies declare their common determination to ensure the reestablishment of the countries suffering from acts of destruction, spoliation, and unjust requisition, and decide to join in devising means to secure the restoration to those countries, as a prior claim, of their raw materials, industrial and agricultural plant, stock, and mercantile fleet, or to assist them to re-equip themselves in these respects.

II

Whereas the war has put an end to all the treaties of commerce between the Allies and the Enemy Powers, and whereas it is of essential importance that, during the period of economic reconstruction which will follow the cessation of hostilities, the liberty of none of the Allies should be hampered by any claim put forward by the Enemy Powers to most-favoured-nation treatment, the Allies agree that the benefit of this treatment shall not be granted to those Powers during a number of years to be fixed by mutual agreement among themselves.

During this number of years the Allies undertake to assure to each other so far as possible compensatory outlets for trade in case consequences detrimental to their commerce result from the application of the undertaking referred to in the preceding paragraph.

III

The Allies declare themselves agreed to conserve for the Allied countries, before all others, their natural resources during the whole period

[1] Quoted from H. W. V. Temperley, *A History of the Peace Conference of Paris,* Vol. V (London, 1921), pp. 367–369.

of commercial, industrial, agricultural and maritime reconstruction, and for this purpose they undertake to establish special arrangements to facilitate the interchange of these resources.

IV

In order to defend their commerce, their industry, their agriculture and their navigation against economic aggression resulting from dumping or any other mode of unfair competition the Allies decide to fix by agreement a period of time during which the commerce of the enemy powers shall be submitted to special treatment and the goods originating in their countries shall be subjected either to prohibitions or to a special regime of an effective character.

The Allies will determine by agreement through diplomatic channels the special conditions to be imposed during the above-mentioned period on the ships of the enemy powers.

V

The Allies will devise the measures to be taken jointly or severally for preventing enemy subjects from exercising, in their territories, certain industries or professions which concern national defence or economic independence.

C

PERMANENT MEASURES OF MUTUAL ASSISTANCE AND COLLABORATION
AMONG THE ALLIES

I

The Allies decide to take the necessary steps without delay to render themselves independent of the enemy countries insofar as regards the raw materials and manufactured articles essential to the normal development of their economic activities.

These steps should be directed to assuring the independence of the Allies not only so far as concerns their sources of supply, but also as regards their financial, commercial and maritime organization.

The Allies will adopt the methods which seem to them most suitable for the carrying out of this resolution, according to the nature of the commodities and having regard to the principles which govern their economic policy.

They may, for example, have recourse either to enterprises subsidized, directed or controlled by the Governments themselves, or to the grant of financial assistance for the encouragement of scientific and technical research and the development of national industries and resources; to customs duties or prohibitions of a temporary or permanent character; or to a combination of these different methods.

Whatever may be the methods adopted, the object aimed at by the

Allies is to increase production within their territories as a whole to a sufficient extent to enable them to maintain and develop their economic position and independence in relation to enemy countries.

II

In order to permit the interchange of their products, the Allies undertake to adopt measures for facilitating their mutual trade relations both by the establishment of direct and rapid land and sea transport services at low rates, and by the extension and improvement of postal, telegraphic, and other communications.

III

The Allies undertake to convene a meeting of technical delegates to draw up measures for the assimilaton, so far as may be possible, of their laws governing patents, indications of origin and trade marks.

In regard to patents, trade marks, and literary and artistic copyright which have come into existence during the war in enemy countries, the Allies will adopt, so far as possible, an identical procedure, to be applied as soon as hostilities cease.

This procedure will be elaborated by the technical delegates of the Allies.

D

Whereas for the purposes of their common defence against the enemy the Allied Powers have agreed to adopt a common economic policy, on the lines laid down in the Resolutions which have been passed, and whereas it is recognized that the effectiveness of this policy depends absolutely upon these Resolutions being put into operation forthwith, the Representatives of the Allied Governments undertake to recommend their respective Governments to take without delay all the measures, whether temporary or permanent, requisite for giving full and complete effect to this policy forthwith, and to communicate to each other the decisions arrived at to attain that object.

INDEX

Index